SCARECROW STUDIES IN YOUNG ADULT LITERATURE
Series Editor: Patty Campbell

Scarecrow Studies in Young Adult Literature is intended to continue the body of critical writing established in Twayne's Young Adult Authors Series and to expand it beyond single-author studies to explorations of genres, multicultural writing, and controversial issues in YA reading. Many of the contributing authors of the series are among the leading scholars and critics of adolescent literature, and some are even YA novelists themselves.

The series is shaped by its editor, Patty Campbell, who is a renowned authority in the field, with a thirty-year background as critic, lecturer, librarian, and teacher of young adult literature. In 1989 she was the winner of the American Library Association's Grolier Award for distinguished service to young adults and reading.

1. *What's So Scary about R.L. Stine?* by Patrick Jones, 1998.
2. *Ann Rinaldi: Historian and Storyteller,* by Jeanne M. McGlinn, 2000.
3. *Norma Fox Mazer: A Writer's World,* by Arthea J.S. Reed, 2000.
4. *Exploding the Myths: The Truth about Teenagers and Reading,* by Marc Aronson, 2001.

Exploding the Myths

The Truth about
Teenagers and Reading

Marc Aronson

Scarecrow Studies in
Young Adult Literature, No. 4

The Scarecrow Press, Inc.
Lanham, Maryland, and London
2001

SCARECROW PRESS, INC.

Published in the United States of America
by Scarecrow Press, Inc.
4720 Boston Way, Lanham, Maryland 20706
www.scarecrowpress.com

4 Pleydell Gardens, Folkestone
Kent CT20 2DN, England

British Library Cataloguing-in-Publication Information Available

Library of Congress Cataloging-in-Publication Data

Aronson, Marc.
    Exploding the myths : the truth about teenagers and reading / Marc
Aronson.
       p.   cm. — (Scarecrow studies in young adult literature ; no. 4)
    Includes index.
    ISBN 0-8108-3904-0 (alk. paper)
    1. Teenagers—Books and reading. 2. Young adults—Books and
reading. 3. Youth—Books and reading. I. Title. II. Scarecrow studies
in young adult literature ; 4.
    Z718.5.A76   2001
    028.5'5—dc21   00-061948

To Sasha,
Who will surely tell me
what I get right and wrong
when he reaches teenage

Contents

Foreword *by Bruce Brooks*   ix

Acknowledgments   xiii

Introduction   1

1   "The YA Novel Is Dead" and Other Fairly Stupid Tales   7

2   The Three Faces of Multiculturalism   13

3   The Challenge and the Glory of YA Literature   19

4   The Journals Judged   25

5   How Adult Is Young Adult?   31

6   We Have Nothing to Lose but Our Isolation   39

7   When Coming of Age Meets the Age That's Coming: One Editor's View of How Young Adult Publishing Developed in America   51

8   Exploring the Basement: The Artistic Challenge of YA Literature   65

9   What Is Real about Realism? All the Wrong Questions about YA Literature   79

10   The Power of Words   85

11 The Myths of Teenage   99

12 Calling All Ye Printz and Printzesses   109

13 Puff the Magic Dragon: How the Newest Young Adult
    Fiction Grapples with a World in Upheaval   123

14 What Is YA, and What Is Its Future: Voice, Form, and
    Access—A Dialogue with Jacqueline Woodson   129

Index   139

About the Author   146

Foreword

In the essays that follow, Marc Aronson—author, editor, and critic of literature for young adults—manifests the quality that should matter most to those of us who work within the exciting freedom of this literature for these exciting people: the quality of respect. As is only right, Marc's respect for YA books is only secondary to his primary respect for young adults themselves. Someone who does not share the fundamental conviction that these are people of profound integrity, intelligence, and feeling ought to be a writer, editor, publisher, critic, librarian, or bookseller for someone else. Young adults deserve our best regard and our best literature.

Throughout Marc's pieces run the same bywords, often implicit, that inspire his work as an editor and author. Subtlety, adventurousness, trust, openness, and curiosity meet with questions as well as answers. Fittingly, young adults are themselves exemplars of these qualities. Marc and the legion of sympatico non-YAs in the field are not the only people who appreciate this. Our young readers can winkle out of the first page of any narrative the slightest sign of condescension, preaching, overtness, distrust, or any of the betrayals we bigshots sometimes put into play.

What happens when a young adult reads evidence of such attitude? I asked my teenage son Alex the fate of a book like this. What do he and his friends do?

"Chuck it," he said.

As for the author or purveyor of the book? "Well," said Alex, "it's going to be harder to trust the person next time."

Do we really want to curry mistrust in the young adults who make it all the way to opening one of our books amid the distractions and difficulties of twenty-first-century life? Of course not—and we could not do better than to consider from all angles the sophisticated stewardship Marc Aronson proposes in these pieces. On second thought, I must say that stewardship sounds a touch condescending itself, or at best stuffy; I have never heard Marc put down his joy and creativity long enough to hoist such a serious scepter of a word.

Joy and creativity thread through these essays—Marc's own, certainly, but more widely the joy and creativity he urges as an impetus for writers, readers, nonreaders, librarians, teachers . . . in fact, for everyone who cares about YA lit.

Hmm, but can any of us afford to get smug about how cool we are at celebrating joy and creativity? Have we never dismissed an ambitious novel of intriguing characters and fascinating plot by saying things of which we should be ashamed—things more appropriate to a "focus group" planning a book expressly to entertain the vast group of average readers, without confusing or ruffling them?

Yes, we hear such dismissals, often uttered with a rather haughty air, as if these standards came down the hill with Moses. "But average thirteen-year-olds don't talk like this!" That's a favorite (as if anyone could verify the way thirteen-year-olds talk to each other in private—or as if that mattered). Another favorite is something such as, "If the corn is as high as he says in chapter 2, the stalks would be too tall for him to see his sister across the field in chapter 6!" Really, how small-minded is that?

The same goes for shielding young adults from words, concepts, and feelings we frankly hope they are too unsophisticated to handle. Why do so many of us seem to want to read a YA book simply to detect niggling errors of accuracy or "inappropriate" vocabulary—whether too difficult or too dirty—in tiny parts, instead of reading a book as a whole to feel how exciting, poignant, or provocative it is. (Provocative, by the way, is good.)

Said simply, it's as if we want average readers to stay average readers, as if we consign them to a place where curiosity or a broadening range of interest could not possibly raise them a notch. Stay down there and be content! If you don't see your limits, we do, and we'll show you a nice, safe way to grow—well, kind of—within them. If we don't look out, we'll all be literato-Leninists, telling the proletarians how lucky they are to be ignorant.

Perhaps I make my point here in a tasteless, disrespectful way. Sorry. But where is the taste and respect, for both author and reader, when a good novel is junked because it has "bad" words in it, inclines the reader's inquiry toward "bad" subjects, stretches out a layered story the reader cannot snap shut at the end like a change purse, speaks in dense language as tough as it is lyrical? Because, hey, this happens pretty often, and to some of the best writers of our literature.

Lucky for literary types, people like Marc keep questioning the more stolid attitudes that might hold sway. Marc challenges the arrogance of judging books because "we adults just do not know any kids who are exactly like the kids in this novel." Marc's writings show that if we chuck such books we are removing from YA readers encouragement to expand their experience of character, to be enthralled with lives and emotions unlike their own.

Other essays take on the tendency to coddle books when the answer is, Yes, we do know kids who match. Marc has heard the YA readers who say, "Yeah? So what?" and trade their Average Kids Just Like You! books for Stephen Kings and Philip K. Dicks, full of telekinetic ax-murderers and autistic aliens.

However, the good news is, we can all save ourselves. We already possess the intelligence and commitment; otherwise we'd be reading *Curious George* to smiling kindergartners instead of deviously pressing *Gypsy Davey* or *Speak* into the reluctant hands of eighth-graders who shave and play in punk bands. Professionals in the field of literature for young adults are, as a group, enthusiasts to the point of nuttiness. Marc is not always a nut, but he can be pretty intense. Lucky for us, he is also a fine thinker and writer, fine enough to jack up the intensity of our own enthusiasm, leading to new ideas, keener sensitivity, old faiths, and greater enjoyment of books and the young adults who do or do not read them.

And guess what? As he respects young adults, so Marc respects us big shots. In this book there is plenty of what lawyers call committed advocacy, but no condescension, preaching (well, not much), overtness, or distrust. In short, here's a book you will not want to chuck. A young adult could say no better.

—Bruce Brooks

Acknowledgments

M y special thanks to Patty Campbell for suggesting this book and for asking intelligent questions and making insightful suggestions as I worked on it. We don't always agree, but I always profit from the depth of her knowledge of young adult literature and her commitment to books and their passionate readers.

Earlier versions of the chapters in this book appeared in the following places. The author thanks the original publishers for their cooperation and, where relevant, permission to use the previously published essays in this volume.

Chapter 1: *School Library Journal,* January 1995.
Chapter 2: *ALAN Review,* Spring 1994.
Chapter 3: *ALA Booklist,* April 15, 1997.
Chapter 4: *Horn Book,* July/August 1997.
Chapter 5: Speech given to the American Library Association, June 1997.
Chapter 6: *VOYA,* June 1998.
Chapter 7: *VOYA,* October and December 1998, and a speech presented on October 22, 1997, at *Adolescenti e Letture Seminario Internazionale.*
Chapter 8: Speech given at "Radical Change in Children's Books" conference at Florida State University, June 1998.

Chapter 9: Speech to Westchester County young adult librarians, Spring 1998.

Chapter 10: Speech given to New York State Library Association Conference, Spring 1997.

Chapter 11: Speech to "Teenagers and Reading" conference, New York, March 1999.

Chapter 12: Speech to Michigan State Library Association, November 1999.

Chapter 13: *Los Angeles Times Book Review*, September 1999.

Introduction

This collection tracks a decade of issues and trends in books for teenagers through the talks and essays of one editor of young adult (YA) books. That can seem like a very small window on a small corner of the world, even if it is the world of writing, publishing, and reading. But the issues I discuss are really the effects of significant and large-scale causes. For the place where reading and adolescence cross is dependent on society's definitions and redefinitions of coming-of-age, as well as how—in an era where the Death of the Book is announced with startling regularity—we define reading.

I entered the world of YA literature in the 1980s, which was a particularly embattled time for the genre. As I discuss in some detail in chapter 8, the fading of YA began with a declining teenage population that was matched by a national revulsion against the "don't trust anyone over thirty" mood of the 1960s. This slide toward extinction was sped along by shifts in publishing, bookselling, and library budgets that increasingly favored books for children and consigned anyone over fourteen to adult books. As many of the essays in the first chapters show, the question then was whether YA could, or even should, survive as a branch of literature. Those pieces were a plea for space and for recognition, as well as a call to arms for the faithful to have hope in a dark period.

Through the course of the 1990s teenagers, slowly at first and then with ever greater force, returned to the national agenda. Once teenagers were back, I had to consider who we imagined these strange creatures to be. It is as if a banished people were returning to the light, which meant that we had to examine who we had always believed them to be. In those essays I make the case for treating YA literature as a branch of the arts, not as part of a program of mental or moral hygiene. If YA books should be appropriate to teenagers' state of development, does that mean their main function should be to help readers grow up? Is YA a helping function designed to lead readers on to adult books? Or is it a literature in its own right?

Now, in the wake of both the Littleton shootings and the success of shows such as *Buffy the Vampire Slayer*, teenagers are unavoidable. Every form of media is scrambling to capture their attention. The later chapters in this book grapple with the problem of success. Now that we have the Michael L. Printz Award for Excellence in Young Adult Literature, popular Teen Read Week promotions, the *Teen People* book club, and recognition for teenagers and reading in every national magazine, what should a YA literature be? It is clear that teenagers exist and that they read, but what is really distinctive in YA literature?

Reading over the essays to be included in this volume, I was struck by this arc from lonely battles to nearly limitless horizons. But I also suspect that there was a deeper change going on in American society—a kind of tectonic shift—whose effects we are only beginning to see in print.

As I understand it, in the 1970s—the real crucible of YA literature—nearly half of Americans lived in nuclear families anchored by a married couple. The challenge of adolescence, you might say, was to face your sexuality, your rebelliousness, your aspirations in a way that would allow you to reach dry land in your twenties. If you negotiated these crosscurrents well, without making any bad choices that had life-defining effects (such as giving birth or landing in jail or contracting a terrible disease or struggling with your sexual orientation), you would find a life partner of your own and begin a new family.

Many YA novels recorded the strain of trying to complete this passage in families that were themselves under strain. One of the most significant developments in American society is that we have changed our opinion on how to deal with those family pressures. Divorce, recombined families, single-parent families (which are linked to the rise in women's income and reduced pressure on women to define themselves through marriage), alternate types of family, including same-sex parents or extended families in which grandparents provide child care, are no longer the tragic end of a family drama. Instead, they are normal variations, the new sites of new kinds of coming-of-age.

Today (according to statistics I once saw crawling across my screen on CNN's *Headline News*), about a quarter of Americans live in nuclear families with children, while 18 percent are in single-parent families. The 1970s world has nearly split in half. What does this mean for the challenge of adolescence? In one sense, I suspect, a decrease in pressure. A teenager who experiments is not in much danger of destroying her future, since it is very likely that she will spend her twenties, and perhaps her whole life, continuing to explore new options. If the pill gave rise to sexual experimentation, in vitro fertilization encourages trying out whole new ways of living—since the biological clock can nearly always be rewound.

In the world of *Sex in the City* (HBO's sitcom series about successful New York women in their thirties who can keep making new choices about their partners with little fear of losing out on future family life) teenagers may have less sense of a tightrope with dire consequences for a misstep. But there may also be an anxiety that comes with this free-form future. Where *is* the dry land? How do you know that you've reached home, when a marriage may end or change form at any moment?

As some of the later chapters show, this idea of a future of multiple narratives has now become as familiar a part of YA literature as the old books that centered on a single problem that held promise of a single solution. Adolescence is, by its nature, a kind of learning-by-doing in which experiencing adult feelings challenges young people to try out adult roles. As those roles shift, the literature that explores this territory must also change. That is one reason it is so interesting to watch and ponder.

Another theme in many of these essays is the gulf between the aims of creators and the credos of evaluators of YA literature. Artists, acting as dowsers, as distant early warning radar, sense the changes in adolescence, but the world they publish into moves more slowly. YA literature is embedded in the school and public library world; many who judge YA bring to it conceptions of teenage, and of reading, that change much more slowly than does the actual experience of teenagers. Others seek to evaluate this literature by arcane standards that have long been abandoned in adult criticism: popularity, morality, utility, ethnic purity, accessibility to average readers. A final set of critics—those who populate the standard general interest review organs—ignore YA literature entirely and only notice coming-of-age books when they are published for adults.

Throughout this book I try to examine, to test beliefs and attitudes that I see in the criticism of YA books. Out of sight of the general trend of adult criticism and buttressed by the beliefs and needs of parents and teachers, critics of YA have too often enshrined opinion as law, projection as insight, myth as truth.

There is something about teenagers and reading that encourages elevating half-truths to sacred writ. Perhaps because we adults fear teenagers or because we feel we have the right to think for them, they are often used as counters in our arguments. We speak confidently about their likes and dislikes, we opine knowledgeably about the rules for reaching them, we argue fiercely about their receptivity to the good and bad "messages" in books. But we rarely if ever question how we know all of this. Throughout the book I contrast my certainly limited but ongoing experience in hearing teenagers talk about books to our adult "rules."

Which leads to the other part of the link of adolescence and reading I mentioned in the first paragraph. A central question that runs through these chapters is whether or not teenagers are reading at all.

One of the most frequently repeated announcements of the 1990s was that we were at a paradigm shift, a Gutenberg moment, in which digital connections would replace the individual text and interactivity would rule. Teenagers are a perfect test case, for they are the first generation in which many were computer literate before they could read. If they are not reading books, books surely are a doomed, outdated technology. And if teenagers' behavior disproves the jeremiads, then—as another set of essays asserts—we adults must question why we were so wrong.

Montaigne invented the modern form of the essay. He chose that term because he saw this genre as a kind of test, an assay, in which he would pose challenges to himself and see where the attempt to resolve them took him. That is the spirit behind every one of these pieces. Observing YA literature from inside, I raise questions about what I see and probe to find out if the answers I've heard are really sufficient. Time and again I come to the conclusion that they are not—that we settle for answers about teenagers and literature that do not honor the true depth of the readers or the true potential of the literature. I am sure that I have been right to ask these questions, to pose these problems. I am not at all sure that I have better solutions to offer.

If there is one single message in this book, it is that we must all be on guard against the complacency that tends to surround YA books—whether in announcing their demise or celebrating their triumph. And that surely applies to me as well as to anyone else. I hope that reading this book will provoke you to ask more questions, to challenge my conclusions, to push on to new ideas. That will constitute success, for a chronological collection shows change over time, and YA literature by its nature is in a constant state of change. If you leave this book puzzled, turning ideas over in your mind, seeking new answers—posing your own tests—you too will be in a state of change, which is perhaps the best state to be in when thinking about teenagers and the books written for them.

1

✚

"The YA Novel Is Dead" and Other Fairly Stupid Tales

This 1995 essay records an interesting transitional moment. Advocates of the CD-ROM seemed to hold the future in their hands, yet within a couple of years they turned out to be false prophets. YA as it had been defined was on life support, yet new voices were coming to the field giving it new energy. Adults had given up on teenage readers, yet the first teenager had just been smuggled into a Best Books for Young Adults committee meeting at an American Library Association conference. Advocating for a YA Newbery Medal seemed a pipe dream, yet we now have the ALA Printz prize, the *Los Angeles Times* YA fiction prize, and a young readers' National Book Award that includes teenage books in its purview. All this change is a reminder that, in a field as mobile as books for teenagers, we may have to look in unexpected places to see coming trends.

"Teenagers just don't read anymore." "You can't publish anything but junk." "The sky is falling." All of these statements have about the same truth value. They take a nugget of half-perceived observation and turn it into a half-regretful pronouncement. One favorite argument of these prophets of doom is that multimedia products set a standard of color, sound, and interactive fun that no book can match. "We are at a moment of paradigm shift," both hacker apostles and gloomy elders announce, picturing a wired world beyond books. We are due for a paradigm shift, but in entirely the opposite direction: not from books to images but from fuzzy nostalgia about the past to clear-sighted recognition of the present. I think we are at perhaps the most exciting moment for young adult publishing ever.

The service of the now passé problem novel is that it made the shock of recognition—"Hey, I am not alone, other people have felt what I feel"—the heart of YA fiction. That cleared the decks. All possible subjects are now admissible as long as they can evoke that reaction. Up for grabs for the modern YA novel are matters of ethnicity and race, issues of faith and religion, markers of gender and sexuality, problems of home and society, choices of politics and belief, concerns about money and the future. In short, the YA genre now engages the profoundest, deepest, and richest issues that we face as a nation.

At the same time, the very media options that are said to threaten teenage reading have freed publishers to be more creative. A young adult novel may now employ a surrealistic style, a poetic voice, hard-edged realism, or a highly personal blend of interior reflection and exploration of the outside world. It may even be a picture book. We are liberated by our competition, not threatened by it.

Because no topic or style is off-limits, novelists are free to write with as much depth, beauty, and insight as they can muster. Because sexuality with all its confusion is an accepted part of this process, we get groundbreaking books such as Marion Dane Bauer's short story collection *Am I Blue?* and Francesca Lia Block's *The Hanged Man* (both HarperCollins, 1994). Because identity and self-formation are at the heart of YA, an intense, literary novel like Kyoko Mori's *Shizuko's Daughter* (Holt, 1993) has not only been well reviewed but widely read. Because we assume all the world is the canvas of the search for identity, we get unique creations such as Nancy Farmer's *The Ear, the Eye, and the Arm* (Orchard, 1994) or Suzanne Staples's *Shabanu* (Knopf, 1989). Every one of these books is a declaration of independence for the young adult novel.

If the genre is flourishing in its subjects, what about its market? It is ironic that the explosion of children's bookstores created something of a problem for YA. A teenager does not want to be within ten miles of a store called Fuzzy-Wuzzy's, so it is no wonder that the more the retail market mattered to publishers, the worse things got for those interested in older readers, especially since the terms "library" and "cutback" have become almost synonymous. What has emerged from this is a splintering in what we mean by YA.

As Deborah Taylor told those attending a conference on "Teens in Troubled Times" at the New York Public Library, there are two groups of YAs: ages eleven to fourteen, and fourteen to eighteen. The younger end is actually doing fine. They show up in the libraries, they buy books, publishers know they are out there. What's more, the Newbery Medal confers the highest honor in children's writing on books for their age level or below. The older end is the vexing problem. We all recall that as soon as we were able to read adult books, we did. It is easy enough to think that older teens will find their way to adult books, too, and that this readership is too hard to reach in libraries or bookstores anyway. Worse yet, there is no Newbery for older books. That makes it all the more difficult to give such books the recognition they deserve. Still, there is hope.

Our experience with Edge, Holt's multicultural hardcover YA imprint, has been that the single greatest determinant in sales has not been the age level of the book or the characters in it but rather how good it is, how well reviewed, how it stands as art. And that is not true merely for us. More difficult, more multicultural YA novels aimed at older readers from Orchard, Houghton Mifflin, Farrar, Strauss & Giroux, and others are eagerly sought by paperback houses for reprint. They wouldn't pay their good money if they did not see a market. Harcourt is trying simultaneous publications of hard- and softcover editions. That is not an option for all houses but is a sign of inventiveness, not gloom. [*Simultaneous hard and soft publishing has generally not worked. At the end of the decade the new area of experimentation is with trade paperbacks for teenagers, and here results have varied.*]

On the other end of the spectrum, consider the book that gave this piece its title, Jon Scieszka's *The Stinky Cheese Man and Other Fairly Stupid Tale*s (Viking, 1992). This work is not aimed at older or younger teens, not at teens at all. Yet at the 1993 ALA midwinter meeting, a seventeen-year-old got up to plead that it should be voted a Best Book for Young Adults (which it eventually was). He, and many readers his age, got it. They got the humor, the intelligence, the defiance of tradition, the wild wisdom of the book. So really, the question is not, Is YA dead? but rather, How broad, how wide, is its territory? It is nearly oceanic.

If anything died, it may be the restriction, the constraint, the box into which we used to try to fit YA books. Here, too, is where the censorship wars arise. If we imagine YA means a book that inculcates certain attitudes, that preaches specific values, that aids coming-of-age by pointing the way, then we do have something to lament. That kind of book may be a casualty of the sophistication of teenage readers. Although in the endlessly creative adaptability of the marketplace, surely some publisher will start a line of such novels and do well with them. The reality of our multimedia moment is not that teenagers don't read, but that reading is part of a much larger media mix.

Carl Kaestle's *Literacy in the United States* (Yale, 1991) points out that the single greatest correlate for literacy is education. More schooling equals more reading. Whatever harm may come from electronic alternatives is outweighed by the gain that comes from learning. That reading may be a computer manual, a trading-card price guide, *Sassy*, or Terry McMillan's *Waiting to Exhale* (Viking, 1992), but it is reading. My sense is that teenage readers move easily from screen to online to magazine to book to CD to CD-ROM. None rules, but none must. Each has its place. We may not have their unmixed attention as in our fantasy of nineteenth-century readers, but does anything command that focused gaze today? Is not that electronic kaleidoscope the essence of the modern condition? *[This early speculation was confirmed by the market researchers who spoke at the conference on teenagers and reading that I discuss in the introduction to chapter 12.]*

Ian MacDonald's brilliant *Revolution in the Head* (Holt, 1994) argues that the mixed-media, channel-surfing mentality is the product of the 1960s, of the kind of collage of sounds heard in the Beatles' "Revolution Number 9." Why shouldn't modern teenagers read the way we did then: with John Lennon (or Lou Reed or Janis Joplin) blasting out of the speakers; with men walking on the moon and the Mets winning the World Series on TV; with our minds on Cleaver and Leary and Castaneda; our notebooks full of rock lyrics and overwrought poetry about love, death, sex, the pigs, and the coming apocalypse?

Out of that creative frenzy came classic YA authors such as Barbara Wersba, Judy Blume, Paul Zindel, and Bruce Brooks. Not a bad haul for a supposedly distracted generation that had not had time to read because it was going to "save the world." That generation had to fight against limited prescriptions for teenage reading. Its heritage is the exciting moment in which we find ourselves now.

Today the field of YA fiction is not even confined by language. Books in Spanish or Spanglish like Lori Carlson's *Cool Salsa* (Holt, 1994) or Gary Paulsen's *Sisters/Hermanas* (Harcourt, 1993) are well received by both reviewers and buyers. Perhaps the only areas that are out of bounds for YA publishers are impenetrable stylistic experiments that appeal only to academic aesthetes. And, to be realistic, we must cede to adult publishers best-selling cyberpunk, mystery, romance, and exposés that teens enjoy but that YA publishers could never afford to acquire. Left standing as the new YA is everything from graphic novels to gay autobiographies, from medieval romance to Beat poetry, from violent hockey stories to Holocaust diaries, from passionate vampires to African American family histories. As I am sure you know, there is at least one YA book in each of these categories that is available or soon will be.

That list reveals the very opposite of a doomed field. Instead, it shows that we as publishers and you as librarians and reviewers recognize that YA is as varied as the multimedia mix of teenagers' lives, as complex as their stormy emotional landscapes, as profound as their soul-shaping searches for identity, as vital as their nation-forming future. Which brings up a final point. Statisticians tell us that we have passed the moment of teenage turnaround. From now until 2010 there will be an ever increasing cohort entering their teenage years. By that date, teenagers will occupy an even larger percentage of the population than they did in the 1960s. If that makes all of us want to buy more life insurance or invest in Gap stock, it should also show us that finding the voice and echoing the emotions of those readers is more important than ever.

We have the authors, they have their themes, there are ever more readers, and they read. If that sounds like death, I'm not sure what life is. If it seems like wishful thinking, come to an ALA Best Books committee session where the teenagers give their views. You'll see the conviction that can only come from the opinionated, the exercised, the devoted. In the voice of my generation I thunder, "The YA novel LIVES." And in their voices you'll hear the vibrant sound of that indestructible, unstoppable whirlwind of curiosity and passion, the teenage reader.

2

✛

The Three Faces of Multiculturalism

This is one of the first essays I ever published. At that time the "do you have to be it to write it" issue came up in discussions of literature for young readers, but it was not yet an open debate. It was more a felt presence that was feared might crop up in reviews or buying decisions than an articulated position to be supported or opposed. This murky status made it a kind of taboo that was understood but resented. It was as much a commercial warning about what would sell as it was an intellectual argument. Since then it has been hashed over in great detail on listservs such as CCBC-Net and Child-lit. In turn, publishers such as Lee and Low, Just Us, Arte Publico, and the imprint Jump At the Sun have built their lists around a particular vision of authenticity and serving the community.

I include this essay here for a number of reasons. What I defend in the particular case of multiculturalism is really my most general conviction about the self and art: I believe in multiplicity and individuality. As Walt Whitman said, the artist "contains multitudes," and we should be receptive to that, not seek to confine him or her by preset ideas of what literature for young people should be. But we do. And there are many similar taboos that afflict our field to this day. Because we adults are reading for younger readers, we feel very free to define what is or is not right for them. Here I try to show that one such taboo

13

has no intellectual foundation. In later pieces I ask similar questions about many of the other "rules" of YA literature.

An editor I know got a disturbing phone call recently. She was interested in publishing a young adult coming-of-age novel about an Irish Catholic girl and had sent it to a paperback house to see if they might want to buy those rights. The paperback editor, I am told, was angry. She loved it; though neither Irish nor Catholic, she was very moved by the story. Her boss, though, turned it down. "Irish Catholic is not multicultural," she was told with the force of a papal bull. When I heard this story and thought of the Jewish, black, and Hispanic high school I went to—in which there was nothing more exotic than Irish Catholics—I realized it was time to try to define exactly what multicultural means to me.

In a way, the paperback house can be forgiven its foolishness: they were reporting what they find in the market, not what they believe to be true. And, in reality, many reviewers, librarians, teachers, parents, and teenagers do confine the "multi" in multicultural to third world, nonwhite, "oppressed" people. Sometimes they grant a variance for Appalachian poor whites, or for Jews from 1939 to 1945, or—in a triumph of ideological prestidigitation—women. The fact that "third world" is now a meaningless term, "white" erases differences as fatal as Catholic and Protestant Northern Irish, and that the line between oppressed and oppressor shifts radically when, say, you consider what to write about female genital mutilation, somehow eludes the monitors of ethnic purity.

This view of multiculturalism is a political position, not an aesthetic or educational one. It seeks a literature that will challenge the dominant power structure, as one advocate argued at a recent conference of the National Council of Teachers of English. If the world is viewed as made up of a hegemonic, gender-bound, racially and economically dominant power structure and its victims, then it is of utmost importance to have literature by the victims. Their voices serve to undermine a ruling ideology and supplant it with a new one; the guarantee of the "authenticity" of their voices is their membership in the groups they write about. The politics of oppression divides the world and "multi" means "other than dominant." I have a far more radical view to propose. If they split the world into black and white billiard balls, I seek to free the subatomic chaos within both.

Within all of us are stereotypical patterns and inversions of them; we have traits similar to others of whatever set of groups we fit and resistances to them; we both incarnate and transcend the set of characteristics we fit on a census sheet. It is that personal, fluid yet at times explosive, maelstrom that literature can capture. The "multi" in multicultural is, at its best, the many selves within each of us, not our melanin count or epicanthic folds.

Our curse in children's books is to get intellectual trends about ten years behind the times. On this one, let's take a quick leap ahead. The most interesting writing on race, identity, and literature is coming from people like Harvard professor Kwame Anthony Appiah. In his brilliant *In My Father's House* (Oxford, 1992) he makes a startling claim. Though he was born of Ghanaian and English parents and is very deeply grounded in the literature not only about but of Africa, he states boldly: "there are no races." Wading through the biological literature, he shows that there is as much genetic variation within anything called a race as between any two such groups. If there is no single set of physical characteristics in a race, how can history have acted on such people in any defining way? The only possible answer is that race is established by the prejudices of those who seek to define themselves against it. You were black if you had to sit in the back of a bus or live in a township. You are white if your literature is not multicultural. But this immediately means that race depends on who experiences it, and that means it is as personal as sexuality, or imagination. Of course prejudice and oppression do exist but they act on each of us as individuals, and it is that personal experience that leads to the best literature.

We are all on dangerous margins these days, especially young adults. Whether we recently immigrated to America and have to balance traditional ways and media-induced options, or have been planted here for generations and find new peoples and ways either enticing or threatening, we find our identity changing daily. My best friend is from India. When he is around his relatives, his accent becomes more and more subcontinental—which infuriates his Canadian/Indian wife. An author I know went to Korea to find her roots; she came back certain only of her rootlessness. She is Korean but unable to live in Korea; American but not like the images she grew up seeing; Korean American but having to define daily what that means. It is this dangerous, shifting, uncertain world of multiple allegiances that is the heart of multiculturalism. It honors younger readers by not confining them. Let me explain how.

There are three distinct kinds of multiculturalism; though they share similar terms and apparent concerns, they are mutually exclusive. The nature of bipolar politicized multiculturalism was exposed by a recent debate in a journal for professional historians. The contentious issue was whether whites should be allowed to teach black history. Think of the circuit that establishes: only people of a group can write about it or teach it. Should people of other groups even be allowed to read about it? Why? If they read, they may identify, grow curious, seek to become expert, seek to communicate their knowledge, seek to *(gasp)* write or teach about it. What about the children of intermarriages? Do they get a variance? What degree of racial purity is required to listen to the music of another culture? What if, like Don Byron, a black Protestant jazz musician plays Jewish klezmer music? Is that good or bad? Authentic or unauthentic? In the name of authenticity, political multiculturalism turns the reader into a receptacle of ideology, not a creative mind.

The equally damaging reverse form of multiculturalism is the "small world" brand. This paints a picture of other cultures as a series of nicely dressed dolls in quaint native dress all endlessly and tiresomely proving the point that "hey, Juan is just like me. He loves his parents, goes to school, and wants his favorite team to win. But oh that pesky sister Juanita, she's a pain." This form of writing flattens out the very dire, and real, conflicts among and within people, mimicking authenticity by turning the world into a mall. It insults readers and ultimately makes them less interested in other cultures. One of the virtues of political multiculturalism is to expose the poverty of this form of bland earnestness. *[At a more recent NCTE conference a teacher told me about careful study she had done showing that books using the "he's just like me" strategy had the least to say to her students, who instantly got the message and were bored by it.]*

The version of multiculturalism I favor is intensely curious about all cultures in all of their ambiguous, complex, self-contradictory splendor. It glories in new perspectives, other experiences, and different expressions, not for their political or moral value but for their human depth. And for that reason it opens the field to gifted writers of any background. Talent, not the exploded category of race, is its pole star. Authenticity means depth, insight, communicative value, resonance, rigor, care. In that way, it gives (to use a 1960s phrase) "all power to the reader." The reader is the crucial actor ignored, or patronized, by the first two forms of multiculturalism.

The novelist Edmund White made exactly this point in a *New York Times* op-ed piece on December 21, 1993, based on a talk he gave to a gay and lesbian group. "What counts for me," he explained, "is . . . how any book is read by a particular student—with what kind of informed skepticism, critical acuity and historical depth. The mind of a particular student, far from being just one more vessel into which the divine liquor of canonical wisdom is poured, is at the moment of reading the *unique* theater on which Shakespeare's plays are staged. . . . A book exists only when a living mind recreates it."

Pouring ethnically pure, or ethnically bland, literature into student vessels turns education into catechism. The multiculturalism I favor corresponds to and thus frees the many voices in the reader. It encourages her to explore all of her selves: the master and the slave, the male and the female, the black and the white. For that reason, I am as eager to include Irish Catholics in my roster of multicultural experiences as I am Holocaust victims, Namibians, and Latino Americans. After all, for all I know I may have a little Jesuit, or (I wish) Joyce, in me.

3

✛

The Challenge and the
Glory of YA Literature

This essay was written as a piece for *Booklist*, one of the
few periodicals that review books for younger reader
books for adults in the same issue. The problem of findi
borderlines and defining characteristics of young adult
ture runs throughout this book. The essay in this chapter
sents my most thorough effort to work out what I think
subject.

The issue of age and genre connects in another wa
continuing theme of mine: the claims of art versus the
development. Literature for younger readers is a uniq
of art in that it is judged simultaneously by its aesthe
"appropriateness." It is treated as a branch of the a
moral or intellectual education. I applaud that in n
which I think is too often evaluated as a form of fi
the main issue being whether or not readers will en
than for the texture of the author's argument. But
suspicious of it in fiction where, too often, adu
fears, and limitations blind them to authors' acco

What is YA fiction? A genre of its own? A
describes whatever teenagers happen t
lite," a bridge that adolescents cross on their w
This is not just a question about reading mater

are neither children nor adults. Answering it requires u.
with the nature of all books for younger readers. Are th\
tools along a road of emotional, psychological, and intellec
velopment that comes to a happy ending when you can leav\
behind? Or might they be an art form in their own right? S\.
we judge these books vertically, as steps "up," or horizontally\
literatures of their own that have their own rules but are not inhe\
ently better or worse than others?

When thoughtful adults consider picture books, it is not hard for
them to appreciate how they are an artistic genre of their own:
thirty-two pages, thirteen or fourteen spreads, carefully selected language, a form with its own parameters, much like an ode or a sonnet. Parents, teachers, critics can easily see how the restriction poses
an artistic challenge. The very best picture books succeed not just
because they appeal to kids but because they use constraint as opportunity, which is the very definition of classicism.

Classical precision, spareness, and constrained invention—which
leave plenty of room for humor, play, and psychological depth—are
the hallmarks of great books for younger readers. Their emotional
challenge is to treat and evoke the most basic feelings without becoming trite or maudlin. The limitation of space and the necessity
of art make picture books an interesting aesthetic challenge, no mater the age they are intended to serve. But what happens when this
lassical style encounters the storm and stress of adolescence? What
s the artistic form of adolescent literature?

The achievement of great YA literature is that it extends and ap-
ies the spare language, the focused story, the sharply etched con-
cts of younger books to the multilayered, vexing, often ambiguous
uations of the dawning adult world. YA novels seek to capture the
ensity of adolescence, where truth is a pure value, exposure and
recy are constant themes, and readers feel alienation with first
ce. Classic YA novels describe a great crossing, where a person
ose values and character have been formed in the smaller world
amily, school, and native social environment enters a wider
ld. He or she may be pulled or pushed across this line by per-
l needs such as desire or fear; by intellectual curiosity or grand
ition; by spiritual yearning; or by large-scale social, political, or
omic events. As characters measure the public world by the val-
f the family and reexamine the family in light of new truths
d in the world, they begin to work out their individual sense of
ity; they "come of age."

In the best books, the emotional purity of the picture book becomes the moral fervor of the YA novel. When this fails, it turns into didactic moralism, imposed by the narrator on the characters. When it succeeds, it captures the innocent passion of adolescence, when a child begins to see the secrets, the ideals, and the desires that will give depth to his or her own character and provide a roadmap of the wide world.

The tightrope of adolescent literature is to be true to this period of awkward intensity without descending into awkward melodrama. Books that fail this aesthetic challenge (however popular they may be) mistake overdrawn subjects—incest, anorexia, sex in all its forms and impulses, violence—for heightened experience. Books that succeed may embody the crises of adolescence in seemingly small choices, like whether or not to fake in a basketball game, not just in artificially inflated confrontations.

At precisely this point—the small acts and large feelings of adolescence—we run into the difficult boundary between coming-of-age literature published as YA and similar books that are considered adult fare. Adolescence is the only nonadult time of life that is the subject of an extensive adult literature. Many adult novels and memoirs begin in childhood, but only as the initial stage of a long journey. A book that never leaves teenage can be fully adult. This seriously blurs the question of the nature of YA literature.

On the one hand, adult publishers often shy away from manuscripts that perfectly capture an adolescent voice unless the books have some marquee quality: a famous author, a hot genre (such as Asian-American or African-American or gay), or an attention-getting extremity of experience. On the other hand, a hallmark of the best adult coming-of-age books—works like Jamaica Kincaid's *Annie John* or Lisa Shea's *Hula*—is that they distill adolescent experience and inflect even the smallest acts with an adult's sense of tragedy and depth. This does not necessarily mean such books are set as recollections. Rather, there is a weight and resonance in events that come only because the author is no longer the character: she knows where the shadow she is casting ends, and we adults sense that along with her.

Either version of adult coming-of-age novel describes events or emotions that are a part of teenagers' lives, but in a style not aimed at those readers. What should we consider these books? Clearly, works such as James Joyce's *Portrait of the Artist as a Young Man* (B. W.

Huebsch, 1916), Carson McCullers's *Member of the Wedding*
(Houghton Mifflin, 1946), or, classically, J. D. Salinger's *The Catcher
in the Rye* (Little, Brown, 1951) speak to teenagers. That is why they
are assigned in classes and have continued popularity. Because teenagers read them and they deal with adolescent themes, they fit in
the descriptive field of coming-of-age literature. But they clearly do
not fit within the genre called YA: the subset of books for young
readers that are aimed at adolescents.

It is one thing to recognize that certifiably adult coming-of-age titles can make up a significant part of teenagers' reading lives. It is
quite another to decide how to categorize books that arrive at a publisher as such adult books and wind up being called YA.

Because adult publishers have two very different agendas for
coming-of-age fiction—hot topic versus literary precision—there are
wonderful books that fall between the cracks. These subtle evoca-
tions of coming-of-age either cannot find an adult publisher or
would only appear with little fanfare from small houses. As an editor of young adult literature, I am often thrilled to discover these
books. The very quality that makes them a slight misfit for adult
lists—quietness, purity of experience and voice, truth to a teenager's
experience—makes them very high quality and literary YA.

But the fact that well-written books about adolescence can find a
home on YA lists does not mean they "truly" fit that category. Is a
publishing accident forcing us to squint as we jimmy, slide, and
crowbar books into slots that they really don't fit? If we follow the
developmental model of children's literature, this must be so. These
older books were not written "for" teenagers. Their authors did not
pay any attention to the constraints of language, understanding, or
treatment that some think a younger readership imposes. In reverse,
if we imagine all of children's literature as helping stages that lead
to adult books, having teenagers read books that are "too good"
might arrest their development. They may stay trapped in a younger
literature ghetto even as they become adults. If YA literature is defined as the genre that makes it easy for a teenager to recognize his
or her own experience, or as the style of writing that ushers those
readers on to adult books, these sophisticated YA books certainly
are out of place.

Neither of these models matches the reality of how teenagers read
or how books for them are published. If the aesthetic of YA is spare
intensity, these older or crossover coming-of-age books often add an
additional layer of subtlety that is not so much a part of teenagers'

daily experience as it is a part of their dawning self-awareness. It is precisely because these books straddle adult and teenage that they are appropriately part of the literature of coming-of-age. They are just as suitable for teenagers looking ahead as are picture books, fairy tales, and trading-card reference guides for those looking back. Teenage is a Venn diagram of intersecting experiences and literatures. These older books are one of the sets that extend into adulthood—as do popular adult novels, science fiction, romance, and horror. All of those genres, though, are published as adult books. Why, of all the crossover sets, should certain coming-of-age books be called YA?

In bookstores, subtle coming-of-age books would never last on the shelves long enough to be found by teenagers. Hardcover adult novels have two to four months to prove themselves on bookstore shelves. And very few teenagers can afford to buy them. That means the entire support for these books has to come from adult buyers or librarians. While general librarians with YA responsibilities do pay attention to adult lists, can we really expect them to devote enough of their tight budgets to such books to sustain them? Are we are prepared to say that purchasing books for older teenagers should be entirely an adult librarian's responsibility? I see no such groundswell among YALSA members.

Though the YA sections of libraries and publishers' catalogs are relatively recent creations, they exist. It is far more plausible that we continue to publish, review, and shelve this ambiguous form of coming-of-age literature as YA (with occasional crossover listings) than that we can convince adult publishers, reviewers, and librarians to suddenly keep in mind potential teenage readers. After all, not a single general interest newspaper or magazine regularly reviews YA books—precisely because they all believe that no teenagers pay attention to their reviews. Would calling more books that teenagers might read "adult novels" change their minds? Not likely. Coming-of-age fiction published as adult would be dismissed as too "small" or "quiet" instead of being termed too "young," as it is today.

Instead of waiting for "crossdown" publishing that will occur occasionally at best, we should accept that we are dealing with a complex series of unstable categories. Teenagers read widely, at times revisiting favorite books for children, at others exploring sophisticated literary experiments. If we use the term "young adult" to mean a sociological description of this reading world, we have to consider the full range of both children's and adult publishing. Even considered as a literary term, young adult literature contains at least two distinct categories: the "true YA" genre of books in which teenagers can easily recognize themselves and the adult-inflected literature of coming-of-age I have just described.

This confusion of styles, subjects, and treatments is not merely the challenge of young adult, it is its essential nature. It forces us to keep pushing at the boundaries that confine YA: keep asking adults to pay attention to subtle books that deal with adolescence; keep inviting teenagers to read books that treat coming-of-age in a sophisticated manner. This effort honors the mixture that is adolescence by creating a fluid literature that mixes "up" and "down" with the very freedom, experimentation, passion, and—yes—awkward uncertainty that is the glory of being a teenager.

Coming-of-age literature is an overlapping set of art forms, all of which keep pressing against their boundaries. If this forces us to keep questioning ourselves and redefining our terms, that is just as it should be. The literature that deals with coming-of-age should be just as engaging, perplexing, complex, and changeable as the stage of life it describes.

4

✛

The Journals Judged

It is interesting to look back at the moment when the field of books for young readers in general, and for young adults in particular, first began to get some attention from the larger literary world. Since *Harry Potter*, that mission has been accomplished. But it is still difficult to get serious review attention for young adult literature.

On the night of November 4, 1996, an overflow crowd of agents, authors, and publishers packed a midtown Manhattan auditorium to listen as the National Book Award nominees read from their work. The event began with Carolyn Coman reading the opening scene of her novel *What Jamie Saw* (Front Street, 1995). From that moment on, there was just one topic in the buzzing crowd: the amazing and totally unexpected talent of the five nominees in the young readers category.

"I didn't know you could do that in a kids' book." "Those certainly weren't the books I read as a child." And, sotto voce, "You know, they really were the best." Sweet as it was to hear these comments, this night of triumph for the modern children's book was also an implicit indictment. If the reading was the coming-out ceremony of coming-of-age writing, it also showed how carefully sealed off this literature has been.

This gap between the quality of what is being written and what the world knows is the fault of the reviewing system that judges

25

children's books. The daily papers, the Sunday review sections, and the weekly or monthly magazines pay halfhearted, impossibly delayed, or summary attention to the field. Occasionally the *New York Times Book Review* will feature an article by a Kwame Anthony Appiah that poses a needed challenge to facile multiculturalism, or one by a Katherine Paterson that wrestles with the place of virtue in children's books. But these are rare exceptions.

No children's book author can count on getting that kind of considered reception in these publications, and both young adult novelists and all nonfiction writers should not even hope. Of the five National Book Award finalists, only *What Jamie Saw* received a full and timely review in the *Times*. *Send Me Down a Miracle* by Han Nolan (Harcourt, 1996) has yet to be reviewed, while the other three—the Newbery Honor title *A Girl Named Disaster* by Nancy Farmer (Orchard, 1996), the eventual winner, *Parrot in the Oven* by Victor Martinez (Harper, 1996), and *The Long Season of Rain* by Helen Kim (Holt, 1996)—were mentioned, a minimum of five months after they were published in tiny "bookshelf" listings. No wonder no one outside of the insular children's book world had heard of them.

If general interest publications pay erratic attention to children's books, children's book journals pay scant attention to general readers. The established review publications are not oriented toward the ever-more-influential retail market. They cannot engage with the literature in a fashion that could draw the attention of intellectuals interested in an evolving art form, nor can they—with the exception of a lead article or editorial—offer an extended critique of art and text that might engage artists in a creative dialog.

The sole task of children's review publications is to advise school and library professionals on buying decisions. That is a fine and noble function, though—as I'll soon show—the magazines are having trouble fulfilling it. The larger problem is that the literature is now too varied, too sophisticated, too extensive to be served by that kind of criticism alone.

Some of the best children's writers and artists are experimenting with new styles and formats. When you know the intelligence, sensitivity, and daring of some of these creators, it is heartbreaking to see the entire critical response reduced to a few long-delayed paragraph-long notices. I'm not complaining that the reviews are too negative; indeed, the critical ones are often the most thoughtful. Rather, I am lamenting the disproportion between the time-consuming, risk-taking invention of the artist and the tiny space given to criticism.

Why not judge these books as part of the evolution of modern art, not merely as tools for children? Many reviewers are quite open to new styles, daring language, unfamiliar topics. But the best they can offer as acknowledgment is a box, pointer, or a star, which are somewhere between a classroom head pat and a guarantee of better sales. That does not take the place of an extended encounter with the work.

Even we who work in children's books often fail to realize what is going on in the literature that we all create and judge. We are participating in the evolution of some of the most interesting art forms of our time: the thirty-two-page picture book, the heavily illustrated nonfiction text, the young adult novel. Were these adult forms— think of the nouvelle roman, hypertext, or gonzo journalism— critical publications all across the land would be discussing, celebrating, evaluating the achievements. On those rare occasions when a children's book artist (such as Maurice Sendak) or author (such as Virginia Hamilton) is recognized by the adult world, exactly this kind of discussion follows.

Artists need that kind of intellectual challenge and guidance— think of the roles Clement Greenberg and Meyer Schapiro played in the development of abstract expressionism. Ambitious critiques of that sort would also draw the attention of general readers to the field, who could look at the books as art, not just as kids' stuff.

But those who are charged with the critical examination of children's books are bound by their mission: to assess utility and popularity and to advise on institutional purchasing decisions. Nuanced art criticism and earnest, literal-minded needs assessment are just not the same.

Even this kind of broad-ranging review would not serve the largest and most neglected group that is concerned with children's books: parents who buy books in stores. Parents need timely, engaged, thoughtful reviews that can help them buy presents, school aids, or leisure reading for their children. Bookstore buyers are an increasingly dominant segment of the children's book market, and they are not served by any publication.

The most recent effort to reach parents, *Children's Book Review*, struggled to finds its readership and is now defunct, while *Horn Book* and *Publishers Weekly* are sold in small numbers in bookstores.

Parents, faced with aisle after aisle of spine-out middle grade novels, and a tiny assortment of current YA publications, have no idea which book to purchase, why one is better than another, or which book missing from the shelves they should request.

Publishers, who have come to realize that they cannot count on the review system to guide retail sales, have placed increasing reliance on other means to sway buyers: jazzy covers, famous authors, heavily promoted series, sure-bets, tie-ins to holidays, or niche marketing tied to events such as Black History month. Because established reviewers who have the knowledge to help parents have no way to communicate with them, the field of children's books is developing largely without their aid.

In theory, the institutional reviews could help parents, but to do so they would have to overcome several serious handicaps. Because they are oriented toward schools and libraries with long buying cycles, journals such as *School Library Journal, Booklist, Bulletin of the Council on Children's Books*, and *Horn Book* have not traditionally placed a premium on timeliness. Getting the review right was more important than getting it promptly. But chain stores give children's and young adult books limited exposure. After a season, one set of books is gone, replaced by another. If a parent cannot find a book, it does not matter how positive any review might be.

Just this spring, some publications have sped up their reviewing. But those in the industry still hold their breath when a book is published. They wonder whether it will be reviewed, when, and by which publications. We just cannot trust a system of reviewing that is not oriented toward our largest group of customers: parents who need a review if and only if the book is in the store. *[The journals ebb and flow; by 1999 late reviews had become an increasingly severe problem. I know of one book reviewers received in the summer of 1999 that was not reviewed in two leading journals until the following March.]*

A second failing of the institutional reviews is their brevity. Three hundred words is not enough space to give any serious work serious attention. This is made all the worse by the responsibility reviewers feel to signal buyers about any potential controversy the book might arouse.

A reviewer who is guiding library purchases feels constrained to indicate anything in a book that might cause problems about "authenticity," "offensiveness," sexuality, language, or religion. As a result, complex disputes over the nature of literature, which have consumed American criticism since William Dean Howells and Henry James first wrestled with Emile Zola's realism, are reduced to coded hints that shift a book from a necessary purchase to an optional one.

This kind of criticism once again marginalizes the institutional reviews. Authors and publishers, furious that the fate of a book is decided by reviewers who make sure to nod to all possible political or social critiques, look for other ways to promote their books. Parents, who are unfamiliar either with the history of American criticism or the disputes within the children's book world, cannot possibly know whether the reviewer's hints mean this is a really bad book, a slightly bad one, or a good one to which only some extremists might object.

Finally, there is the matter of personalism. Perhaps in the name of directness, some reviewers allow themselves to be totally unprofessional in how they express their judgments. Last fall, for example, a *Kirkus* review of Helen Kim's *The Long Season of Rain* summarized the emotional dynamics in a traditional Korean family this way: "passive-aggressive (the men), narrow and manipulative (the women)."

The use of snide Western pop-psych terms to describe Korean emotional dynamics would be questionable at a cocktail party. It is immoral in a published review. It does violence to the trust we place in reviewers to take their charge seriously. Imagine the hue and cry that would arise if we published a book in which a character mouthed the same words. One hundred percent of the reviews would describe the terms as culturally inappropriate. Fortunately, other reviewers saw the book differently. In addition to the NBA nomination, Kim's book was selected as a best book of the year by both *Publisher's Weekly* and *School Library Journal*.

At one time, many people viewed children's books as a publishing backwater. Novels that were too thin or programmatic to pass muster as adult books were sent over to kids' departments as possible YAs. Nonfiction that was easy to read, not terribly thorough, or not too burdened with complexity was deemed "just right for children." Reviewers stepped in to demand higher standards of art, more thoroughly researched nonfiction, folktales whose lineages we could trace.

Now, due to that criticism, as well as the pressure of competition, many children's books aim higher. But reviewers have not kept pace. General interest publications cannot get over the ageism that confuses a younger-than-adult subject with a lesser-than-adult level of artistry, talent, or ambition. In the institutional world, some reviewers are so timid as to be preoccupied with anyone who could be offended by a book, while others are so offensive as to be unreadable. None offers either the timely, concrete information parents need or the wide-ranging engaged criticism that an expanding, artistically inventive literature deserves.

Books for children and young adults are too good, too varied, too fast-growing a literature to be served by a system of reviewing that is characterized either by dismissive high-handedness or earnestness with a very limited focus. If this year's NBA reading, and every other one after it, is not to be a repeat of last year's damning triumph, it is up to the reviewers. You speak about this literature, now you must speak for it, and to the great wide world. *[A number of readers objected that this essay slighted the work of the thoughtful critics whose essays, editorials, columns, books, and talks take this literature quite seriously. I appreciate the work of the critics whom all readers of this book can name as rapidly as I could, but this piece is about a structural problem in the nature of the YA review system, not those standout individuals who, from time to time, manage to defy it.]*

5

+

How Adult Is Young Adult?

This piece was a speech I gave at a panel that Michael Cart organized for the American Library Association conference in 1997. That very well attended meeting in New York was a watershed moment, an evaluation session, and a self-help group in which all of the battered lovers of YA got together, saw how many of us there were, and began to have hope that the field could revive. The advocacy and struggle that led to the Michael L. Printz Award—though it surely had many other antecedents— really began there.

Recently, while preparing to teach a course on children's publishing, I had occasion to read through a number of histories of children's literature. I learned many things from this—including how little we really know about the subject. But I was especially attentive whenever the subject of writing for teenagers came up. And what I saw in, say, Michael Cart's book *From Romance to Realism* (HarperCollins, 1996) or Betty Carter's *Best Books for Young Adults: The History, the Selections, the Romance* (ALA, 1994), was how difficult it is for us to decide what young adult literature is.

YA literature sounds like a descriptive term, but it is actually an agglomeration of instabilities. It requires us, simultaneously, to define three inherently unstable terms: what are young adults, what is literature, and what is the literature that has some special link to those readers. And yet, day to day, we all act as if we knew what YA meant—books for readers aged twelve to eighteen.

What, or who, are young adults? Sounds like a simple question, but it is not at all. Both Cart's and Carter's books go back to 1930, when librarians started making a list of "Books for Young People." Who were these "young people"? They ranged from people interested in adult books to those served by an elementary school librarian. To shift from the very vague and capacious term "young people" to "young adults" required a general acceptance of the idea that there is a separate stage of development called adolescence. When did that begin? And what is that stage?

The *Oxford English Dictionary* offers one rather quaint suggestion: "the process or condition of growing up . . . the period which extends from childhood to manhood or womanhood . . . ordinarily considered as extending from 14 to 25 in males, 12 to 21 in females." Nice of them to be so precise. The *Encyclopedia Brittanica* is cleverly more evasive, which only deepens the problem. It announces that the term "is a convenient label for a period in the life of an individual (approximately ages 12 to 20); such usage need make no commitment regarding the character of adolescent development or the specific nature of its causes (e.g. pubescence)." The entry goes on to say what is by now obvious: "authorities are not in agreement as to the nature of adolescence."

So we have approximate age boundaries—which we note do not correspond to YA as defined by publishers, schools, or libraries—in which something happens, which may have something to do with puberty, but we're not sure what. As both Michael and Betty know, this is further complicated because we have become increasingly aware of the history of human development and the cultural construction of identity. In other words, if all kids eventually go through puberty, not all of them experience recognizable adolescence.

Were girls advised by elders and guided through coming-of-age ceremonies in which they embraced their reproductive role and even their sexuality? Or were they sternly told to manage their desires, with ever greater control as the sign of dawning maturity? Depending on how young people are reared, they may or may not go through what we call adolescence. Here, I must say, I disagree with Michael Cart. He cites studies that locate the beginning of adolescent culture as we know it in the postwar years. But if you read specialized histories of adolescence, the picture blurs.

The culture of young people, associated with rebellion, cliques, outrageous behavior, and sexuality, flourished in the 1920s in the colleges—though it was muted in the 1930s by the Great Depression and in the 1940s by the war. And even before that, "young adults" in Paris in the 1830s were notorious for having long hair, wearing colorful medieval clothing, using drugs, listening to wild music, having affairs, and mounting various barricades in the cause of revolution. We call those rebels "bohemians," but their most salient characteristic was their youth.

According to John Gillis in his *Youth and History* (Academic Press, 1981), it was during this period in Paris that young adulthood was born. People needed a phase of life between being children at home and adults with careers. Because of the rise of cities, industrial capitalism, and state bureaucracies, there was an increasing disruption between being a child and being an adult. Thus "young adult." Of course the bohemians were mainly in their early twenties, but Rimbaud, often considered the first true avant-gardist, was sixteen when he wrote his best poetry. In his words and his life he more or less predicted everything we associate with rebellious adolescence. Here's one line: "I will make gashes over my entire body, I will tattoo myself. . . . you will see, I will howl in the streets. I wish to become quite mad with rage." Walk over to Saint Mark's Place in the East Village and you'll see this vision of life enacted over and over again by young adults.

I found all this out researching my book on the avant-garde, and the more I looked into it, the more of a link I saw between challenging art and that challenging time of life, young adulthood. If, then, we leave the question of what young adult and adolescent means with some idea that within the last 170 years we in the West created a space for non-children, non-adults to test themselves against society, each other, and themselves in some mix that includes sex, thought, conformity, and rebellion, we still have the question of what is the literature that speaks of and to that stage.

What do Baudelaire and Rimbaud have in common with Sweet Valley High and Judy Blume—this year's Margaret Edwards Award winner? Here Cart and Carter are helpful; they show how a category that initially included mainly adult books came to encompass a new literature about and aimed at teenagers. They describe a particular moment in the 1960s, when "the moon was in the seventh house and Jupiter aligned with Mars, when peace guided the planets and it was the dawning of the age of" YA. Specifically, there were more teenagers than ever—about 20 percent of the population in 1970, versus 14.5 percent twenty years earlier—there were new issues for teenagers—sex, drugs, politics, and rock and roll—and there was new money for libraries.

LBJ's Great Society dollars meant that libraries could easily acquire the books they needed. Thus librarians put up signs reading "Young Adult," filled the shelves with a mix of counterculture authors like Carlos Casteneda and Eldridge Cleaver, chroniclers of dark adolescent breakdowns like Sylvia Plath, and an increasing number of "true" YA titles like *Go Ask Alice* (Simon & Schuster, 1971), and watched readers stream in.

Once this category existed in the libraries publishers began to expand their list of titles to fill it. As new authors like Judy Blume explored new areas that teenagers enjoyed reading about, the bookstores also were eager to feature YA titles in paperback.

For a time, people had a pretty clear idea of what YA literature was: problem-driven novels that allowed confused kids to feel that they were not alone with their angst. Be it sex, pregnancy, suicide, homoerotic desires, incest, AIDS, anorexia, scarring, heroin, coke, interracial romances and clashes, divorce, or even, later in the 1980s, aging hippie parents who were lost in their own battles with these same issues, there was a book for it. And they sold well. Sales were enhanced by the growth of chain stores and children's bookstores, both of which could tack on a small YA section to hold the popular titles everyone wanted to pick up.

This moment of success is the tragedy of YA publishing. Despite all the uncertainty about both the nature of adolescence and the literature that serves it, we have frozen our terms around a late 1960s reality that no longer exists. First, from the 1970s to the 1990s we hit a YA demographic trough, such that in 1990 YAs were down to 14 percent of the population, the lowest number in forty years. Second, federal money for libraries dried up. And third, the media that surrounded adolescence expanded and changed both its form and its substance. Between talk shows, the Web, and MTV's simulacrum of *The Real World*, every human relationship, desire, affliction, and abuse is public knowledge. No one needs a book to tell them they are not alone.

While these social changes were taking place, an important shift occurred in publishing. As adult divisions came under increasing pressure to produce frontlist big books, they felt more uncomfortable or uncertain about books whose strength was a nonadult, or adolescent, voice. When such a book came in, no matter how well written, an editor would say, "Not for us, but send it over to juvenile, don't they do YA?" So, filtering in to kids' divisions were books written as adult novels that just happened to take as their subject something having to do with coming-of-age, and, due to the author's skill, really captured the tone and mood of a teenage character. These were called YA but had nothing in common with the problem novels and series books that dominated the field. Authors like Bruce Brooks and Robert Cormier came to YA in this way and carved out their own niches. But it was an awkward alliance, and two late 1960s events made it an impossible one.

In an unexpected way, the year 1965 had a big role to play in the future of YA literature, as did 1969. Changes in the immigration act in 1965 significantly altered the cultural composition of our country. For the first time a broad range of Asians and Latin Americans began arriving here. By the 1980s, the immigrants were acculturated enough to begin writing about who they were, and their children were experiencing the cultural conflicts that come with being a teenager. Coming-of-age literature, then, became a very broad category including everything from the Cultural Revolution to the making of Women Warriors to life in a House on Mango Street.

After Stonewall in 1969, there was a similar opening up in gay and lesbian literature. Here again the coming-of-age theme, tied often to the coming-out theme, was at the heart of a very rich body of work stretching from memoir to novel. Obviously, in these post-Terry McMillan days, where the month of February stretches before both libraries and bookstores as a great absence waiting to be filled, African American coming-of-age literature is also growing.

So here we have the fate of YA today just as the demographics tilt again and YAs are on the rise: we have library sections that are used by readers from about eleven to fifteen or sixteen; we have bookstore sections aimed at readers up to about age fourteen; we have a genre of literature defined by what it was about twenty years ago; and we have an ever expanding set of authors and subjects that cannot be shoehorned into these categories. There are ever more teenagers who read, and ever more writers dealing in challenging and interesting ways with teenage life. But how can they be brought together?

Our experience in books for older teenagers at Holt may be something of a model. Our most successful books—Kyoko Mori's *Shizuko's Daughter* (1993), Lori Carlson's *Cool Salsa* (1994), Jacob Boas's *We Are Witnesses* (1995), Nikki Giovanni's *Shimmy Shimmy Shimmy Like My Sister Kate* (1996)—have succeeded by crossing markets. They reach YA and Asian American adult, YA and Latino adult, YA and Jewish adult, YA and African American adult. Or at least that's what the sales patterns show.

My sense, then, is that we may be doing ourselves harm by calling books YA that deal with older teenage life or deal with coming of age in a sophisticated way. Perhaps, recognizing how historical and contingent adolescence and young adult literature are, we ought to split both our library collections and our bookstore sections in half. Books aimed at readers up to age fourteen should stay were they are, as a kind of outer fringe of children's books. But books aimed older should be in a new section that blurs teenage and adult, coming-of-age as experience and as memoir, fiction relating to ethnicity and fiction of the Gen-X moment.

This section, which might include magazines, music, electronics, T-shirts, college guides, backpacking manuals, extreme sports photobooks, zines, and so on, would be closer to what those dictionary and encyclopedia entries mean by adolescence. It would recognize that seventeen and nineteen have more in common than seventeen and fifteen. Once such a section existed, publishers could publish into it, whether the books were acquired in kids' divisions or in adult.

So far we've been looking at YA from the teenage side, but it is equally a problem for college kids. Last year I had a chance to teach creative writing to some undergraduates. Nearly all of their work turned on the standard coming-of-age themes of sex, drugs, politics, and identity. I encouraged them to read Francesca Lia Block and Kyoko Mori as well as Toni Morrison and Edmund White, and they were thrilled to find these new voices.

The section I am proposing would give a comfortable space for teenagers reading up, undergraduates reading down, and all adults fascinated with coming-of-age themes. It would celebrate this time of life as one of the richest, most passionate, most dynamic periods of development instead of disguising it as some uncomfortable addition to, or perversion of, childhood.

I recognize that creating such a section poses problems for both stores and libraries. Stores are essentially split: kids' sections are oriented toward families, and adult sections toward individual browsers. This section would have to make room for packs of teenagers. Libraries, in turn, are hampered by the artificial split that comes at eighteen, when readers pass out of one librarian's domain into another's, even if the reader's interests continue to range wildly.

Maybe, then, we should ask for some intermediate steps: YA nights in bookstore cafes, a YA Newbery from the library world, YA books released from publishers with the kind of support and enthusiasm given to adult titles. Perhaps they should even come from adult divisions. A group of YA publishers has been testing out the idea of putting out a zine with samples of our latest fare. I'm hearing from many teachers, librarians, and reviewers who are making creative use of the Web to link teens to books, to each other's writing, to interested adults around the country. Any and all of these ideas have potential. But whether we change how the books are published, sold, displayed, promoted, reviewed, and/or discussed, we have to think in new ways. [*YALSA is now collaborating with publishers to get galleys of YA novels to teen reading groups.*]

Young adulthood is an unstable term for a period of life characterized by wild and uncertain swings between being a child and being an adult. In turn, the literature about this phase ranges over many styles and includes some of the topics of greatest interest to adult authors. All that remains rigid and unbending is our outworn set of categories. What an irony it would be if all this history produced irrelevant designations that throttled a thriving form of literature just as ever increasing numbers of children came of age and adults searched for literature that described their own life-shaping identity struggles.

But it doesn't have to be that way. If we approach the editing, marketing, cataloging, and sales of books about coming of age with the same invention, ingenuity, and passion as we see in our readers, we should have no difficulty solving this small problem. YA is dead: *Long live YA!*

6

✝

We Have Nothing to Lose but Our Isolation

This piece and the following one were occasioned by an international conference on teenagers and reading that I attended in Rome in 1997. This essay is a summary of what I learned from the editors, authors, teachers, and librarians from other countries who spoke there. The following piece is my own speech, which offers a potted history of YA in America.

We were late. My wife and I were meandering through the narrow, winding byways of Rome, searching for an obscure little street. San Paolo alla Regola was clearly marked on maps, yet we kept getting lost as we stumbled through the maze of ancient roads and medieval plazas. Truth to tell, some of this confusion came from our own mixed intentions. Measured against the pleasures of Rome, just how important was it to arrive on time at an international conference on teenage literature? All the more because the small library we had to reach was on the edge of the Kafkaesque Jewish ghetto, hard by the alleys with hip new shops, nestled near the rows of furniture restoration workshops—all of which seemed to have both great treasures taken from the palaces of decaying noble families and exceptionally tawdry fakes. How could we not stop to gape at the bas relief of a roaring lion, linger to sample the best espresso in

Rome, or peer through archways into courtyards that hinted of great families with their secrets, their great art, and their dread power?

Delay as we did, once we arrived at the library, I experienced one of those epiphanies so dear to problem novels: we Americans think we are alone in our anxieties over teenagers and books, but we are not. All around the world, authors, teachers, librarians, publishers, parents, and surely teenagers themselves are struggling with the same issues. I went to Rome to tell them how the Americans invented YA literature, and I left thinking about how much we have to learn from the Europeans.

My lessons began when we finally reached the unremarkable plaza. We dashed into an even more nondescript low building and ran up the stairs past one empty floor to the bustling central library for children. It was hard to make sense of the space. We kept glimpsing odd squares where the plaster was missing from the walls, and yet the library sported a Web-access computer, nice new shelves, a playroom for younger children, an international selection of books and magazines including some old standards of the Tom Sawyer/ Jack London variety and some very recent novels, and even an innovative graphic novel section. Scampering to register, find our hosts, and get settled, I kept getting mixed signals: we were late, we were early, this was a tiny, poorly funded operation, this was an amazing international conference that provided simultaneous multilingual translations.

We shouldn't have worried. Though we arrived late by the clock, the conference ran on Rome time. The 100-member audience was just gathering, and the organizers were more eager to hear that we had enjoyed their city than concerned about starting late. And, as we eventually learned, even the missing plaster was a sign of the building's historical importance.

The building that housed the library had been built as early as the medieval period, and in the basement archaeologists are just now cleaning frescos that were painted during the Roman Empire. They are taking samples of all the walls to be precisely sure of the dates. This unprepossessing building in an obscure piazza is yielding unique insights into the lives of common people in the Eternal City.

There was something perfectly appropriate about holding a conference about today's most ignored common people—teenagers—in a library that was established just a year ago and yet is housed amid ancient artifacts. For there were two themes that kept coming up throughout the discussions: America invented the YA novel, and the rest of the world adopted the forms and subjects of those books from us. And yet Europeans, whose understanding of culture, self, and society is grounded in much older and richer traditions than ours, can help us to see YA literature in new ways.

I had been asked to come to Rome for this conference by an amazingly intrepid librarian named Litticia Tarantella. Since I was coming the longest distance—joining other speakers from England, Germany, Sweden, France, and, of course, many parts of Italy—I was to have a central place in the program, leading off on the second day. The first day, though, set the tone.

We were launched into the discussions by an official from the city of Rome, who spelled out the all-too-familiar issues: teenagers are flooded with information, yet how should they make sense of it? How can books be interjected into the media mix, especially when teenagers have only limited access to them, depending on what is available in schools, libraries, and stores. This problem is particularly acute in Italy, since there are no school libraries. But the social structure it points to is exactly the same as ours: Teenagers are both uniquely vulnerable to the assault (or siren call) of every form of media, and yet they have highly restricted access to books. Adults choose their school reading, select the books for their libraries, and stock the bookstores. And yet adults have much less control over every other kind of art, information, and culture teenagers experience daily. Under those conditions, why wouldn't books become marginal to teenagers?

Roberto Denti, a librarian from Milan who has a wealth of experience dealing with younger readers, sounded a note that would return frequently from all of the Italians—they read less than anyone else in Europe. He related this to the conference, since he sees a crucial shift from middle grade to high school. For the younger readers, books are a status symbol. They read to impress each other. He gave an example of a boy who always asked for short books. One day he came in and requested a 1,300-page Stephen King novel. Why, Denti asked, the sudden shift? His eyes twinkling, the boy replied, "Simone won't kiss me unless I read it."

In middle school, groups of readers, mainly girls, pass messages to each other about books. Books, you might say, help define the group; they give it some common currency. This group embrace of books makes the library a comfortable place. But in high school this world of identification through reading is broken up. Students move on to different schools. As solitary readers they have to make their way through adult collections. They are disoriented. This is all the worse in modern Italy, where students from a greater variety of backgrounds are now going to high school. In the past high school was dominated by teenagers from elite families who had their own strong sense of culture. Now the student may be leading her family into education. She may have no one in her family to turn to for reading advice or suggestions.

In one sense Denti was describing a difficult and frightening fall-off from the comfort of friendship and family to the isolation of adolescence. But he also saw it in the opposite way. Teenagers are becoming autonomous as individuals and as readers. That is healthy and good. But it puts a particular strain on YA literature.

Teenagers, Denti so accurately observed, want books with subjects, style, and even pace that corresponds to their own world. They feel this all the more strongly because their school reading is so far removed from their lives. Italian high school students are compelled to read true classics such as Homer, Dante, and Petrarch. And their parents are upset about books that deal with such modern and controversial topics as rape. The world teenagers see every day in the media is not represented in the books they read. And the newspapers and review media pay scant attention to contemporary books for adolescents. Adults, then, are a barrier to teenage reading, not an aid to it. This leaves teenage readers feeling all the more alienated and isolated.

Summing up, he found a deep gap between the social world of middle school reading and the alienation of high school. The only hope he saw was for adults to try to keep in touch with teenagers' interests. Teenagers are in the new media world; that is their reality. If adults want books to be part of teenagers' lives, they must provide books that are equally attuned to the present. If teachers or other adults object to the content of such books, Denti would remind them that the real goal is to get teenagers to enjoy reading. That is fundamental in itself. Not because books will teach better values or create better behavior, but because reading in itself is a good.

Allowing for some national and cultural differences, Denti's speech sounded like a particularly thoughtful version of a thread that might be found on YALSA-BK, the listserv for young adult bookish topics sponsored by ALA. His attention to the sociology and psychology of group versus individual, identification versus autonomy, was great. The next speaker brought the matter even closer to me. Francesca Lazzarato is an excellent editor at Mondadori and knows everything there is to know about publishing books for teenagers. Her speech addressed the world of YA from an Italian publisher's point of view.

Italy, she feels, is a Catholic country that has valued the visual over the literary. Illiteracy was, for many in power, a good, not an evil. When authorities—whether Fascists or Catholics—have promoted books for younger readers, these have been texts heavily laden with moral messages. The legacy of that is the low literacy rate and the lack of school libraries. As an editor, she must continually search the world for books to translate. She had found the German and Eastern European books for younger readers too didactic. That means she turns to English-speaking countries such as Australia, to Latin America for magic realists, to Africa and Holland for books to translate.

The quality she values in the texts she buys is that the reader can enjoy the book for itself, not for its moral or educational value. She publishes such books in paperback, which again makes them cheap enough for a young reader to buy. Much the largest segment of teenage buyers comprises twelve-to-thirteen-year-olds. Echoing Denti, she noted that at that age readers influence each other. For older teens, she has developed a new imprint called Supertrends. Here she has very limited printings of 3,000 copies but takes risks in subject matter. The books may deal with family crises, cultural clashes, sexuality, ecology and the environment, racism and tolerance.

I kept hearing everything Lazzarato said in reverses. After spending days in awe of Rome's visual density, the richness of its layering of images, it was hard to see that as a cultural failing, especially as so much of the talk in America is about how the digital generation is becoming more visual. More middle schoolers now probably know at least one meaning of the word "icon" than college students did a generation ago. The internationalism of her list is a reminder of how provincial we can be. And yet it was refreshing to have a speaker reading in a larger historical context. Her struggle against institutionalized illiteracy and heavy-handed moralism have given her a hard-won appreciation of how the best YA fiction works.

A book may have morals or messages in it, for the reader to select, absorb or reject as she chooses. The book does not compel the reader to a given conclusion but respects his independence and allows him to piece together his own values. As books respect teenage readers' autonomy (that word again), they also reflect teenagers' passions. When adults react against these books, they are not protecting teenagers, they are protecting themselves. What we deem appropriate comes from our own concerns and interests, not those of teenagers. Because we know our own lives are flawed, we want books to set a better example than we can.

All of adults' efforts at control are undermined by how teenagers read. Exposed to multimedia, and—as Denti noted—coming from a wide range of class backgrounds, they are subversive readers. Knowing this, in her Supertrend books Lazzarato allows no censorship. She knows this keeps the books out of many libraries and even bookstores aimed at children. But based on the letters she gets from older teenagers, she knows the books are read avidly.

Lazzarato's publishing program sounded like Old Home Week, and I was pleased to see some very familiar faces on her list: Anna Novac's *The Beautiful Days of My Youth*, Leslie Beake's *Song of Be*, Melvin Burgess's *Smack*. Publishers around the world are facing some apparently irreconcilable truths: we must publish books for older teenagers, and these books will offend some adults who act as guardians of reading, so we are sure to have low sales. Perhaps international successes like *Smack* will point in a new direction. Even if each publisher only sells a few thousand copies, older teenagers around the world may begin to read the same books. A sixteen-year-old in New York may have more in common with his peers in London or Rome than with a twelve- or thirteen-year-old in suburbia.

After hearing Lazzarato's speech, I felt like a delegate to the First International who had just recognized his commonality with the workers of the world. In many countries, it seems, older teenagers are fought over by moralists, educators bound by old curricula, and the mass media. Just as their challenge is to sort out who they are, they are being trapped or seduced by adult interest groups. If we want them to have the chance to discover books that have none of these agendas, our best bet may be to share ideas with our peers around the world.

Appropriately enough, just as I was feeling particularly rebellious, we heard from Anne Pissard Mirabelle, a library consultant and magazine editor from France. France is the home of reason and revolution, of state systems and intellectual debate. All of this was reflected in her report.

This speech contained a series of psychological and anthropological insights into the teenager that I found breathtaking. They were a reminder of the supple, broad-ranging, and rich insights European thinkers have to offer. French studies have found that teenagers do have money to spend, much of which goes to fads and fashions. The way teenagers spend that money is particularly revealing. Doc Martins, for example, were designed as men's shoes. For teenagers, they became woman's wear. Now in Paris, some boys wear girls' shoes. Teenagers use fashion to define who they are and how they are different. Most significantly, they wear clothes that are baggy, too large, designed for others.

In their clothing teenagers are showing both that they want to set their own rules and that they are being placed in roles that do not suit them. By wearing ill-fitting adult clothes, they simultaneously register that they are not adults and also broadcast the adult lives they already lead. A child playing dress-up shows she is a child; a teenager broadcasts a more ambiguous message.

This duality and discomfort with adulthood is particularly evident in the children of baby boomers. This generation of French parents are permissive with their children and perhaps still working out their own Peter Panish affinity with being young. In their clothing the teenagers are showing that they have had to be parents to childish adults and also that they do not feel entirely ready to be adults themselves.

The French are given to studies, with fascinating results. Tests on the effect of TV show no impact on teenagers' reading. As in America, girls read more than boys. Two-thirds of girls and exactly half that number of boys read in their free time. Fifty percent of the girls in the study kept diaries, and only 12 percent of boys. The government is now collecting some of these anonymous diaries and using them to develop models of adolescent development. If that seems quite invasive, it also shows a degree of interest in teenagers that is in vivid contrast to our cross between anxious control and resigned disinterest.

Until the 1970s, French libraries had nothing directed at teenagers. They had stocked classics and standard adventure tales. Now the library seeks to offer tools for young people to build their own personalities. Ninety percent of YA libraries are attached to schools, and almost all offer Internet access. Books are organized by subject, not age.

Mirabelle ended her talk with a success story. One small suburban library ran a mock Goncourt Prize (like our Pulitzer or National Book Award) contest with teenage readers and voters. This was a particularly successful effort to make teenagers' opinions count, and it may be extended to other schools. Obviously it is much like our mock Newberys and other teen reading groups that offer straw votes on literary prizes. Once again, an effort to take teenagers seriously, and to treat their opinions about books as important, worked.

The last speaker on the very rich first day was another knowledgeable librarian, this time from Turin. Carlo Reveli echoed the previous speakers' focus on serving teenagers' own interests. He embraced all the kinds of technology in teenagers' lives, from music to video games. Like a number of the librarians, he used Patrick Jones's *Connecting Young Adults and Libraries* (Neal-Schumann, 1998) as his authority on how to build the new collections teenagers will like.

My wife had skipped a couple of talks and gone out to explore. That night at dinner with our hosts and Dr. Mirabelle she reported on the reverse side of rich European history. She had gone to wander in the old ghetto, until it took her to a modern synagogue. It was Sukkoth, and she was pleased to see Jewish teenagers in the ritual hut built on the grounds next to the temple. But just outside the gates there were Italian policemen brandishing machine guns. Life has gone on after the Holocaust, but the price is that the most normal celebration requires the most vigilant security.

The next day we once again had to scurry to meet the schedule. This time it was more serious, both because we had made that lunch our one truly great blowout meal and because I was the first speaker. Though the cab driver had to use a map to find the library, we again made it before everyone had settled into place.

My talk rehearsed the history of YA in America (see chapter 7). Then Paolo Verri, also from Turin, brought the focus back to Europe. He described some creative efforts to overcome the problems we had heard about. In the citywide Festival of the Book he used music to reach teenagers. Verri brought famous jazz musicians and pop stars to play. Teenagers responded to the lyrics of the songs, showing an interest in literature without even knowing it. By making this a marriage of common interest, not a competition between text and sound, he reached teenagers. Verri also brought in singers who write books, so teenagers could make a direct association between the two media. Then as a series of first novelists came to town and discussed their books, teenagers felt they were part of the mix. They were neither ignored nor segregated out. This was a very rare effort to both welcome teenagers into the general reading population and accept their particular interests and affinities. Stafania Fabri was the first author to speak, and she gave a most evocative talk. She based it entirely on the William Gibson novel, *Johnny Mnemonic*. Fabri is a librarian as well as a writer of many books for middle readers and younger teens. She is quite comfortable with digital technology but also wanted to consider its effect on teenagers. In the novel, the protagonist has memories embedded in him that are not his. That is like the teenager who is defenseless against the media environment that seeks to dominate and use him. Children, she observed, are protected by their parents. Teenagers have to make their own way.

Traditionally, adolescence has been a time for exploring and defining one's own identity. A person's body is changing, and its needs become ever more insistent and confusing. Mastering this undependable body is both a challenge and a chance to discover one's own resources. Technology is altering this totally. Tied into the Web, teenagers are in an odd kind of dream time—they can go anywhere and link to anyone—yet they are also powerless. On the machine, they are in a world where the physical sets no limits. Yet measured against the power of the machines, their own individual will counts for nothing. Everything is virtual and available. The body that the teenager has struggled to master as a way of entering a wider world is now insignificant. Fabri cited Italian psychiatrists who call this an "excessive trespass of physical boundaries."

Speaking with rare eloquence, she called teenagers the victims and the heroes of contemporary society. Technological change is not a choice for them, it is the condition of their lives. This allows them to rise quickly in the digital world, but it means they are experiencing adolescence in new ways.

While Fabri pushed us to consider the almost science-fiction lives teenagers lead, the next speaker had been a teacher for many years, and he brought us back to the very old-fashioned classroom. Domenico Starnone is an author who for many years had been a high school teacher. Teachers in Italy are forced to teach the classics. But the best of them also have a great deal of freedom in how they do so.

Describing a classroom that sounds depressingly familiar, he told

of students feeling suffocated by teachers even as modern life is exploding all around them. In one experiment, he read his students a
famous Petrarch sonnet and asked them to write down what they
thought was going on. Their responses show just how much of their
own world teenagers bring to their reading. While the sonnet was a
particularly dreamlike evocation of beauty, the students wrote very
concrete paragraphs about lecherous old men ogling teenage girls.

This seemed to me a perfect proof of what we had been hearing
all along. Whether we force-feed teenagers great literature (and I
think you can make a case for this) or please them by offering novels
about contemporary life, they will interpret what they read in light
of what they know. That does not mean they reject literature. Starnone found that teenagers liked poetry better than fiction. Like
Verri, he recognized that their affinity for song lyrics is also a kind
of appreciation of poetry.

I was not going to be in Rome the next day, when Ilona Glashoff
from Hamburg was to present her report on German teenagers. Fortunately, she joined us for dinner and was kind enough to give me
an English translation of her text.

The Germans did a three-year study to test the common myth that
teenagers do not read, and that if they come to libraries it is mainly
to hang out.

Ten years of surveys on teenager's leisure time had shown that
reading actually ranks higher than expected. One-third read often,
one-third sometimes, and the rest not at all. Given that high regard
for reading, some of the basic "wisdom" about teenagers and books
had to be wrong.

Through close study of two libraries, the Germans found out that
the problem was not in the teenagers—it was in the libraries. Having
books, and especially magazines, that matched teenagers' interests
was the single most important way to make the library popular with
teenagers. It was not that teenagers did not wish to use libraries, but
rather that they wanted to use libraries that related to them.

In one way the conference had been a magnificent display of national characteristics: the Italians sent singers into schools, the
French analyzed fashion, the Germans did a lengthy and serious
study, and the American talked about changing markets. Yet we did
more than reflect our own cultural backgrounds. Each person
brought a new set of insights into teenagers. If no one had the single

surefire way to link teenagers and books, together we had expanded the ways in which we understand that particular challenge. This should be the first of many such conferences. Not only because everyone should have an excuse to go to Rome, but because we have so much to learn.

7

+

When Coming of Age Meets the Age That's Coming: One Editor's View of How Young Adult Publishing Developed in America

I explained the general context of this speech in chapter 6. Facing such an audience, half of whom were wearing simultaneous-translation headphones and half of whom weren't, was intimidating in two ways: that I was important enough to warrant all the attention and that this sophisticated, multilingual crowd could so easily range among languages. Still, I was prepared, and intrigued at the crowd's responses, which ranged from pointed questions about whether it was truly acceptable to give teenagers books with gay themes to proposals for books to a general sense that we are all in this problem together. I only wish we all had had more time to exchange ideas.

It is a strange feeling to be an American in Rome speaking about literature to Europeans. Amid this city of history and the arts, our world seems flimsy—as if we lived in a stage set providing only an

51

illusion of solidity and depth. And yet it is that very impermanence of American culture that led us to create a young adult literature. Somewhere in the link between the commercial, fashionable, superficial, and yet somehow supple and emotionally true nature of American arts and adolescence, that time of fashion, image, shopping, and spiritual/political/emotional crisis, is both the story of how YA came to be, and some forecast of its future.

The first thing to know about YA in America is that it is paradoxical. Its history is short and well-known, yet opinions vary greatly on what YA is. It overlaps with every other genre of literature, from books clearly for children to those entirely aimed at adults, and yet it has some identity of its own. It is easy to find sections in libraries, shelves in bookstores, listings in publisher's catalogs identified as "young adult," yet the label seemingly refers to different kinds of books. It is the type of books for young people that is closest to adult books, and yet is the genre most invisible to adult eyes. These mixed definitions, assumptions, and conceptions are like a geological record: they hold the traces of different adolescent experiences, beliefs, and buying patterns. Today, just as the largest boom in the teenage population in thirty years is hitting the schools, YA is a fractured field.

The term YA is an odd one; it refers to no clear developmental age group. If anything, it seems to apply to people in their twenties who are just leaving college, beginning careers, and starting families. That is the sense it had when, as a phase of life, people first began using it. That was about the time of the bohemians in Paris during the period between 1820 and 1840. Those artistic and lifestyle rebels defined much of what we associate with not only the experience but the art of adolescence: they were outrageous individualists with their long hair, Byronic affinity for love affairs, passion for drinking out of skulls, and delight in dressing in ways designed to provoke the bourgeoisie. And yet they were cliquish in the extreme, constantly forming "in" and "out" groups, factions with codes, favorite hangouts, and manifestoes. Their art either reported on their own lives or went off into wild imaginative realms. The most famous piece of art to emerge from this world also defined its most central characteristic. When Mimi, the tragic heroine of Puccini's opera *La Boheme*, dies, her lover sings, "My youth is dead."

As Mimi dies, so also does the stage of life she represented—the time of being bohemian. How did that period shift down in age and over to America? Let's skip ahead to the United States in the 1960s. The children of the Word War II generation, that baby boom born in the hope of new life and new opportunity after so much economic pain in the Depression and human suffering in the Holocaust and the war, had now reached adolescence. They had grown up in a strange combination of security and insecurity. Their parents had done well, buying a series of cars and homes in the suburbs and providing them all the TVs and radios, cowboy costumes and Barbie dolls they wanted. But the shadow of the cold war and the Bomb had always lingered. The kids were confident enough to rebel without fearing the consequences, and anxious enough to mistrust the world that had nurtured them.

You might say they were the perfect product of America: the Stage Set. They were now old enough to see behind the props and billboards and to mistrust the patriotic slogans they heard at school and on TV. And yet they had no more solid alternative to present than to pull down the set and to erect another: the hippie playland of Woodstock Nation. This generation was caught between a protected childhood defined by children's books and a wilder world seen in subversive comics; between the Mickey Mouse Club on TV and images of first the civil rights struggle and then the Vietnam war on the same sets. They did not recognize themselves in any of the books then available for teenagers—which were very tame novels of dating at seventeen or becoming a nurse or boys who lived long ago and far away.

Librarians who had these teenagers in their schools faced a problem: there were more and more potential readers, and nothing on the shelves for them to read. Luckily for the librarians, America at the time was both rich and confident. It believed, for good or ill, that enough money, will, and planning could solve the world's problems—whether by defeating Communists in Vietnam, ending poverty and racism in America, or building as many young adult sections as any librarian could want. President Lyndon Johnson provided the money, and the librarians created a place for a literature that did not even exist yet.

At first those young adult sections featured a mix of the adult titles teenagers might like: the trippy weirdness of a Carlos Castaneda, the black rage of an Eldridge Cleaver, the angst and sense of Jungian mystery of a Herman Hesse, the fearless honesty of a J.D. Salinger. Side by side with these titles were books for children or

adults, such as J.R.R. Tolkien's *Lord of the Rings* trilogy, as well as
science fiction by masters such as Robert Heinlein, Isaac Asimov,
and Ray Bradbury. Notice that this collection, whatever the age-
group for which the books were originally intended, echoes what
I've said about the bohemians. It is either about the radical lives of
the readers, or about their wild fantasies.

In order to make sure that these shelves were filled with the best
possible books, librarians created national committees that would,
annually, pick the Best Books for Young Adults. The makeup, goals,
and rules of these committees have changed over time, but what is
important is that all along, they have had to consider both what
they, as educated adults, believe to be the books that would be best
for teenagers and what they learn by discussing such books with
their teenage readers and finding out which are most popular, most
moving, most important in young lives.

One central issue is to define the role of YA literature in this difficult blend of adult judgment on behalf of teenagers and teenagers'
own preferences in the books they talk about, take out of the library,
and even buy. This mix is more of an issue for this age-group than
for any other. Parents buy books for children, and even when they
bring a child into a store with them and ask what the child wants,
the parent is still present as the intermediary. Adults, who have both
more defined tastes and larger wallets, buy for themselves in patterns that all publishers know and understand. Teenagers are in the
most ambiguous middle ground.

Parents no longer feel confident about buying books for them—
unless it is a book for a very specific need, such as to prepare for
school or for some religious event such as a Bar Mitzvah or confirmation, or, if the parent is a certain kind of liberal, to deal with some
of the dangers ahead, such as changes in the body or safe sex. But
teenagers do not have that much money, especially after what they
spend on music, clothes, sports, entertainment, dates, and so on, is
subtracted. Teenagers are in their own world, where they do not appreciate adult suggestion, but they still depend on adults such as
parents, teachers, librarians, and mentors to provide much of the
world of books. The semiannual discussions of the Best Books for
Young Adults committee—which take place at the meetings of the
American Library Association—perfectly reflect this situation and
are fascinating precisely because of the clashes and mixed agendas
that arise. If any of you have a chance to come to America and attend

an ALA conference, I urge you to do so, especially at the one session each meeting in which local teenagers give their opinions of the nominated books.

The YA sections of the libraries were not dominated by adult books for long. Change came for two reasons. First, as the teenagers whose lives mandated the creation of the sections got older, or into more trouble, they started to publish books about their own experiences. A book such as *Go Ask Alice* (Simon & Schuster, 1971) was about a life of sex, drugs, and rock 'n' roll, and the toll it took. It said directly to teenagers: I am you, my story is yours. Soon an entire and flourishing wing of young adult publishing was created around what is called the problem novel.

Each book centered around one particular problem of teenage life and showed the reader that he or she was not alone in facing it. Whether it was being overweight, or having parents who were getting divorced, or falling in love with a person of the same sex, or struggling with drugs, or being a secret alcoholic, or facing child abuse or even incest at home, or being anorexic or bulimic, or cutting crosses on your arm, or running away from home and being a prostitute, or joining a gang, or being suicidal, there was a book whose plot followed very closely that actual experience and, as often as not, provided either models for coping or even listed groups to contact for help. Problem novels also covered many kinds of physical ailments, grave diseases, and life experiences such as the death of a parent or other close relative. They were very much like the booming adult industry of self-help and coping books, but generally in the form of a first-person novel.

It is easy to make fun of these books, and the novelist Daniel Pinkwater did so brilliantly in a book called simply *Young Adult Novel* (Crowell, 1982). But they did serve a function. They created for teenagers a world of literature in their own voice about their own experiences. They defined a territory that, like teenagers' lives, was not childish but did not center on adults. Over the years, it is this kind of book that I have seen most often on foreign publishers' YA lists, but dealing with, say, skinheads in Germany, or the problem of fitting in as an immigrant Muslim girl in London, or being part of the multicultural, divorced parents and blended family mix in Australia or New Zealand.

The second reason for the transformation of the YA section was the creation of the YA paperback. While all of these problem novels benefited from that development, they were only a part of the flood of books that paperbacks made possible. Paperbacks are far from a new idea. They were introduced in America in at least three different eras before they became a real success just before World War II. But it was not until the 1970s that a publisher at Bantam Doubleday Dell named George Nicholson (who is still active in the field as an agent) realized that books for teenagers would be ideal paperbacks. In this cheap and widely distributed form, a whole world of literature flourished. While many of these books did include teenage problems, authors such as Judy Blume, Paul Zindel, Robert Cormier, and Bruce Brooks added real literary quality to the field. They invented a fresh voice in American fiction that teenagers loved.

These novels also tended to be in the first person and often to have a slightly mocking, subversive tone, as the teenage narrator exposed the ridiculous, foolish, secret-ridden world of adults and other family members. They made the strong feelings and often sarcastic tone of a teenager's inner voice into a literary narrative style.

Since these paperbacks were manufactured expressly for teenagers, they looked different from adult books. The classic book of this period absolutely had to have a realistic cover showing characters with whom readers could identify. Though paperbacks were aimed at bookstore sale, librarians soon realized that the best way to get teenagers to use their sections was to stock some of them. Even if the books soon became battered and worn, they were cheap and easy to replace.

By the 1980s, then, the young adult field had mutated from being a library section made up largely of adult books to being a bookstore and library genre with its own star authors, its own familiar forms, even its own design. But then the entire world of books for younger readers changed, and we are still sorting out what that change has meant for young adult books.

In the Reagan era, the initial conditions for YA changed drastically. Now America was sliding down into a demographic trough for teenagers. There were fewer and fewer of them. At the same time, the entire idea of government funding for anything, much less rebellious, hormone-crazed, alienated, and nonvoting teenagers, became increasingly unpopular. As libraries struggled to balance their budgets, YA specialists were some of the easiest jobs to cut. At the very same time, the children's bookstore market was transformed.

Even as the percentage of teenagers declined, a boomlet of very young children appeared. And their parents, the now grown-up hippies who were entering their years of yuppie wealth and concern with family values, were determined that their offspring would have the best of everything, so that they would grow up and go to Harvard and avoid their parents' mistakes. These parents were willing to spend money as never before on children's books. Just as they appeared on the scene, the world of children's bookstores changed. Up to that point, the typical store that sold children's books was—people said with some malice yet also insight—owned by the wife of a wealthy man. She ran it almost as a kind of charity, as a gift for children, and staffed it with retired teachers or librarians who had lifetimes of experience with children and reading.

In the age of entrepreneurs, those small, essentially nonprofit stores gave way to huge national bookstore chains that were perfect for selling books to yuppies with young children. Throughout the country Barnes & Noble and Borders created large family-friendly spaces in which parents could see hundreds of picture books for themselves, where children could listen to story hours, and where it was very easy to find birthday presents, gift books, or school needs.

The chains gave and the chains took away. What they gave was a huge expansion in the number of stores that sold children's books, and a vast increase in the space within those stores to show those books. What they took away was knowledge. Instead of experienced staff, they hired cheap labor. And the area the chain employees liked least was the children's section, where they had to sell books they knew nothing about. This was not so bad with younger books that parents could sit in the stores and read with their children. It was disaster for YA.

For publishers, the combination of the yuppie children's boomlet and the spread of the chains was a bonanza of unprecedented size. In the 1970s and 1980s, the volume of books sold doubled and then doubled again. But these were overwhelmingly books for younger children. Even as publishers expanded their children's book divisions, in the hallways editors kept saying "YA is dead."

No new author, or even the latest book from a 1970s favorite, sold very well. The problem novel began to fade as TV talk shows and supermarket tabloids made the most seemingly private problem—from AIDS to family violence—public knowledge.

Publishers responded to this in three ways: the series, the changing meaning of YA, and the exceptional book. Paperback romance books for adult women readers are hugely successful in America. There have been series books for children since the nineteenth century and mysteries such as Nancy Drew and the Hardy Boys for twelve-year-olds since the 1930s. In the 1980s, publishers created paperback romance series for teenage girls, most notably *Sweet Valley High* (Bantam)—which in time reached down *to Sweet Valley Babysitters* and up to *Sweet Valley University,* and the many efforts to copy them. These series continue to be very popular. They, like the *Babysitters' Club* and *Goosebumps* (both Scholastic) for younger and middle-grade readers, provide a reliable, satisfying, repeated reading experience. They are like a familiar brand name purchase: you read a book because you know what you will find, and yet you enjoy getting this particular version.

The YA series is essentially the voice of the 1970s YA book—the one that convinces the teenager that you are inside his or her world—perfected as a commercial product. A curious thing has happened to them. Though labeled YA, they have become the province of increasingly younger readers. As children grow up in a world where sex, violence, and racism are more public, books written for them lose that edge which makes them seem like a passageway into the hidden world of adulthood. The series books are popular, but with children becoming teenagers, not with the older teenagers whose lives are depicted in the books. As they say in the magazine world, no seventeen-year-old would read *Seventeen.* That magazine is for the thirteen- to fourteen-year-old who wants to know how to look and act cool.

This downward slide in the age of YA had another source, too. Parents have pushed their kids to read ahead, to be ahead of their peers, ahead of their age level. They are proud to say their kids are reading adult books. And with the popularity and wide distribution of adult authors such as Stephen King and V. C. Andrews, it is not hard to find adult books that young teenagers like. The very well-crafted psychological horror of these books provides a kind of thrill to those readers that a once off-limit topic such as sex no longer does.

Another world of adult books that has crossed into YA is fantasy and science fiction. Read avidly, especially, though not exclusively, by boys, these books immerse readers in alternate universes. Some are quasi-medieval, followers of Tolkien. Some, such as the Star Trek and Star Wars books, are out in space or ahead in time, as was the sci fi of the 1960s. Many are very long, include their own unique languages, and require the reader to understand whole new geographies, laws of physics, and particular blends of magic and superscience. As soon as a reader is old enough to manage the small-print 500-page paperback and memorize the exotic vocabulary, he leaves the world of YA behind.

A third kind of book that blurs age levels is the graphic novel. These are fully illustrated comics-style books and magazines, often filled with gore and sex, and blessed with some of the most inventive and creative use of layout and design anywhere. They are much longer, more psychologically complex, and more artistically inventive than comics or picture books. Yet they have very little text. Created in Europe and Japan as well as America, these are sold mainly in comics bookstores or by direct mail. Officially they are for adults. Yet the particular combination of advanced subject, intense art, and easy language makes them very popular with YA, especially teenage males. Recently there have been a few efforts to create graphic novels for younger readers, as well as to include graphic novels in YA library or bookstore sections.

Between the adult books that claim teenagers' attention and the ever younger assumed readership of YA books, libraries have had to make adjustments. Some have started to experiment with splitting their selections for teenagers. The area called Young Adult is really for readers up to fourteen or fifteen. Books for older teenagers, then, might be mixed in with adult books.

As the world of YA has diminished, split off into series and younger books, with readers lost to adult books, it has also been pushed in new directions by the new subjects and authors who have come on to the scene since the seventies.

In 1965, Nancy Larrick informed the guardians of American children's books of something they should have admitted themselves: the world that appeared on their pages was all white. She was right. Not only were there no black characters and no books by black authors for children, every other American minority group, or foreign people in their own countries, was portrayed in a patronizing or inaccurate fashion. With the advent of a true young adult literature, more and more black, Asian, Hispanic, and Native American authors have entered the field. There are gaps, but books now exist that are not only about these groups but written by members of them.

The year of Larrick's piece was also a historical threshold on a much larger scale. That year America's immigration laws were changed. Instead of favoring essentially white immigrants from northern Europe, the laws now made it much easier for poorer, multiracial, and multicultural people from Asia, Central America, and the Caribbean to come to America. The result has been a wave of new immigrants on a scale not seen since the turn of the twentieth century. America is increasingly multiracial, and in the twenty-first century Hispanics will surpass blacks as the nation's largest minority. The fastest growth in the teenage population is among Hispanics, African Americans, and Asian Americans.

This change in the demographics of American teenagers has come just at a time when the literature of America's minority populations has gotten more and more attention. Whether it be a Nobel Prize winner such as Toni Morrison, a best-selling novelist such as Amy Tan, or an immensely popular family historian such as *Roots* author Alex Haley, American literature has gained much of its vitality from its nonwhite authors. This also means that more and more of these artists are writing memoirs or novels about coming of age. Even as the YA field seemed to be collapsing, it gained new vitality from writers such as Jacqueline Woodson, Kyoko Mori, and Victor Martinez—as well as adult authors such as Sandra Cisneros, Alice Walker, and Gish Jen who had a great deal to say to teenagers.

Another change in adult attitudes and literature that has had a direct effect in YA is the increasing acceptance of books about gay or lesbian identity. John Donavan's 1969 book, *I'll Get There: It Better Be Worth the Trip* (Harper, 1969), was the first YA novel to explore this topic. But it remained a very difficult area for publishers until quite recently. Now, as bookstores, advocacy groups, and even high schools devoted to gays and lesbians have proliferated, some of that hesitation has ended. As a result, the field has grown from the problem novel in which the key moment is the revelation of the protagonist's sexual preference to novels that explore a character's ambiguous sexual yearnings, as well as nonfiction series that provide role models of successful and creative gays and lesbians.

One area that has given a surprising boost to young adult literature is poetry. Verse has been out of favor in America for a good long time. It was seen as either incredibly boring, or impossibly difficult to understand. Neither made it a good match for teenagers. But that has changed. The popularity of rap music has made adolescents very conscious of the power of words, rhythm, and rhyme. The revival of the Beat poets as emblems of rebellion, sexuality, and coolness has encouraged teenagers to drink espresso, grow beards, read Kerouac, and recite their own poetry.

Just now, in cafes and bars in the hippest, most exciting parts of cities, poets have been creating a new kind of art called talk poetry. These works are as much performance as written statement and are often filled with obscenity, anger, and pointed humor. Many of these poets use street language, mixed Spanish and English—"Spanglish"—or heavy doses of black slang. Although not that many teenagers actually go to the clubs, they know about them. Because of influences like talk poetry and rap, poetry has become an exciting form for teenagers. One of our most successful YA books is *Cool Salsa* (Holt, 1994), which includes poems in three languages, English, Spanish, and Spanglish. In the summer of 1997, teenagers throughout Brooklyn participated in a project to write their own poetry, and this will be published by the Brooklyn Public Library in a book called *This Beautiful Name Is Mine*.

Teenagers writing and publishing their own work is another possible source of new vitality in YA. Teenagers have been raised on the books I have discussed, most of which tried to make the reader feel comfortable with his or her own experience and voice. It is not so strange that those readers should want to try their hands at it themselves. If an adult can mimic the voice of a fourteen-year-old, why shouldn't that girl try to speak for herself? Her work might appear in print in publications by schools and libraries, in magazines devoted to this cause, such as *The Write Stuff, Merlyn's Pen, New Moon,* and *Teen Ink,* and on the Internet.

The Internet offers many kinds of new opportunities for teenagers and those who publish books for them. On the one hand, a number of library and school systems give teenagers ways to post their works; on the other, we are just beginning to tap its potential as a forum in which teenagers can evaluate and discuss YA books.

Internet book discussion is one of the most exciting developments in YA. You may recall my mention of ALA's Best Book list and how the librarians who select the books are mandated to get reactions from teenagers. Now, more and more schools and libraries are establishing teen reading groups in which readers discuss and evaluate books. What is more, libraries in cities such as New York and Berkeley, California, then post the results of these talks on the Web. Soon enough we will have the possibility of a national conversation among teenagers about the books that are meaningful to them.

We shouldn't be simplistic about this: a good part of such commentary is on the level of "it's good, I liked it" or follows the opinion of whoever is dominant in a given class. Moreover, since partici-
pation in these groups is entirely voluntary, readers' responses are
far from representative of all or even most teenagers. The movement
toward teen reading groups, teen poetry and fiction, and the increasing use of the Internet to give teenagers a public voice has all
of the virtues and vices that I've assigned to American culture
throughout this talk. As a positive, it allows immediate and direct
expression—the way a new fad, clothing style, or song can become
immediately popular. As a negative, it ignores the entire world of
craft that an adult author, critic, or teacher has to offer. It places the
greatest value in self-expression rather than considered creation.

There are, though, some authors who are trying to combine the
immediacy of a teenagers' world in the swirl of fashion and fads
with a high artistic standard. Francesca Lia Block's magic-realist Los
Angeles, Adam Rapp's invented tough slang, Melvin Burgess's hu-
manistic vision of heroin addiction have nudged problem-novel
themes into new artistic territory. In books such as these, and some
of the more subtle books on gay themes such as Michael Cart's *My
Father's Scar* (Simon & Schuster, 1996) we are seeing a new version
of the YA/adult crossover. Now, it seems, these books will be published in paperback as adult books. If older teenagers are being directed to adult sections in bookstores and libraries, publishers will
seed those areas with YA books dressed up to look adult.

The combination of the aging into teenage of the yuppie babies
and the influx of new teenagers via immigration will create a new
flood of adolescents in the next decade that will be larger than the
one in the 1960s whose advent created YA literature. How will they
change the field? They arrive at bookstores whose selections are oriented toward twelve-year-olds and at libraries whose YA sections
stop at fourteen. Yet they have unprecedented opportunity to express their opinions and to communicate with their peers. And, I
suspect, they will have experiences that will be as unlike anything
in print as did their parents.

Out of this combination of absence and access may well come a
whole new set of voices. The new teenage readers may favor new
language choices—perhaps writing in English inflected by Spanish
or Haitian patois or Korean or Chinese, or the special English style
of the Indian subcontinent. They may be especially receptive to ex-

periments in design and layout—as in the graphic novel or the Eye-witness style of nonfiction. Books in combination with Web sites, digital music, or electronic games may arise as a whole new subgenre. As international cooperation in the exploration of space expands, we may see that frontier shift from a site for fiction to a place for not only science but personal narrative. A generation reared on games of electronic quest and combat may well be especially receptive to new picaresque tales about life in the teenage tangle—a new Cervantes and a new Candide for a new time. On the other hand, teenagers who have already read adult horror may seek out new levels of psychological intensity in their books. Perhaps neo-Kafka will speak to them as Hesse did to their parents. Whatever new forms YA takes, I think it will hearken back to its two initial forms: the direct expression of teenage experience and the invention of new worlds as wild, dangerous, and profound as this one feels to the teenagers who are first learning to master it.

And here I have a plea for you: American teenagers do need to hear from their peers from other countries. But we will never bring your books over unless they reach our readers. We need both that immediacy and that level of creative invention. Direct us to any books, published for adults or teenagers, that could translate culturally as well as linguistically. Give us the tools to expand the reading world of American teenagers.

I began by contrasting the history of Rome with the ephemeral nature of American culture. I end by seeing if we can bring the two together. *Sophie's World* (Farrar, 1994) was a much greater success in Europe than in America. That kind of book, which brought the world's most important thoughts to young readers, is much more prevalent in Europe than in America. Perhaps, if we are able to catch the tone and mood and feel of new teenage life—and can then pass that along to you—you will be so kind as to find a way to capture the grand heritage of culture in which you live in a form that we can bring to our teenagers. For if seeing the world as a stage set is a good part of adolescence, so too is grasping those grand ideas and profound insights from which you will build your own solid foundation. So if, as a product of the generation for whom YA was invented, I am excited to see what the new teenagers will force us to create, as an adult I want to ground them in a world beyond themselves, a world as ancient, beautiful, and mysterious as Rome.

8

+

Exploring the Basement: The Artistic Challenge of YA Literature

I gave this speech at the last of the series of conferences on "radical change" in books for young readers that Eliza Dresang and Kate McClelland held while Eliza prepared her award-winning book on that subject. Although I agree with them that the digital world, as well as social change, is altering not only how books are being created but how young people are using them, I wanted to add another important element to our consideration of books: art. In exploring this topic, I continued to try to probe what a YA book offers to teenagers and how it is shaped by the environment in which teenagers come of age.

Everything that we are talking about in this conference—digital connections, changing populations, shifting standards—puts especially tough pressures on teenagers. I want to explore what books, and art in general, have to offer. But in order to do that, I'll have to go on a couple of detours. So bear with me as we define what teenage is and then take a short walk through some haunted lands. In a conference about connections across media and ideas and ages, see if you can follow my own crosscurrents.

I have a friend who moved from New York City to Vermont in

order to bring up her two daughters. Because of this, I see the family only every few months, which creates a kind of stop-motion film of the two girls' aging. They were in town for New Year's Eve, and then I had dinner with them in Vermont a month later. Between the two visits I saw a big change in the older girl, who is now fourteen. Sitting across from her in a Mexican restaurant, I recognized that something new had been added to her personality: a palpable basement.

There it was, a sense of her doubleness, and of the growing weight of her inner life. I don't mean that she seemed furtive. Not at all. Only that as her body matured, a second layer had opened up in her self and I could feel it. You can tell that in the next few years she will both explore that new depth and integrate it into who she is. The self that emerges will be her adult identity.

To me YA literature is all about that basement: exploring it, retreating to it, fleeing from it, and finally, through integrating it into your conscious mind, establishing your adult personality.

But how can it speak to a part of the self that is just coming into view? And, how can it do so in a way that is true to both sides of the teenager: the comfortable well-lit family rooms, and this alluring inner space of dim red lights and haunting shadows?

Another friend who also knows those girls gave me one clue. She said, "When I was a teenager, I lied. I lied and lied." Teenagers who explore that basement of sexuality, of rebellion, of doubt about the world of adults that surrounds them, lie. And they are aware that they are lying. The contrast between where they are beginning to go both psychologically and physically and their old nice-kid self seems too extreme to describe. This is true even if their parents are completely open and accepting because there is something inherently personal and private about these explorations. The child was part of the family; the teenager who is entering these inner regions is becoming an individual. She knows that what she is doing is fundamentally a betrayal. She is Persephone leaving her mother for Pluto, leaving the floral surface for the deep echoes of the underworld.

We have to respect that privacy. It is bound up with the sense of danger and excitement that comes from entering territory that has been forbidden and is opening up for the first time. The fright and yearning that come with that fundamental shift are real, no matter what attitude parents take. Without those emotions, there is no basement. One paradox of adolescence is that teenagers are both deepening themselves so that they can become full adults, so that they can participate as self-conscious individuals in the public world, and at the same time they are becoming more private and hidden than ever before.

Teenagers lie not just because the rigidity of adults forces them to, but because, up to this point, they knew adults as two-dimensional caregivers or rule makers. As they explore their own dawning adult desires, emotions, and perceptions, they see those same adults in a new way. They see behind those cutout fronts to the frustrations, yearnings, and compromises of adult life. One kind of lie pretends adults are still those nice people—who couldn't possibly understand or accept where the teenager is going—the other holds back from telling adults how the teenager now sees them—the desires, frustrations, conflicts that leak out from behind the mask of adult composure.

After talking about lying, my friend got to the heart of this second challenge of teenage: "Those were the hardest years of my life, because it was the first time when I began to put together the narrative of my life. Before then, no matter what happened one day, I could start over the next. As a teenager I remembered." Even as they are exploring new feelings, teenagers are recalling old ones and weighing who they are. That is why many of them reread childhood books, savoring a self they know they are leaving behind. Just as they question who they are now, teenagers are establishing a sense of personal history. The contradictions of their lives push them to want to create a narrative of being and becoming. And just as they sense their own betrayal, they compare adults' ideals and behaviors, and they feel betrayed.

This time of exploration, privacy, and betrayal is a very fertile one for teenagers' own writing and for literature. As the poet Liz Rosenberg says in an anthology of poetry for teenagers called *Earth-Shattering Poems* (Holt, 1998), "Teenage is often the only time when people write poetry." And, even more commonly, teenagers keep diaries. Lying and narrative, secrets and literature are linked in those pages, which are sealed with a lock. You might say that adolescent literature is keeping a diary in the basement—or in the attic.

Of course that's Anne Frank's *Diary of a Young Girl* (W. W. Norton, 1957), one of the most popular books for teenagers. But think also of all of the real and fictional diaries that are published for girls in their early teens. The *Dear America* series (Scholastic) and the *Ameri-*

can Diaries series (Aladdin) are using this format to go through all of America's past. The classic format of many YA novels—the first-person narrative—is often an extended version of a "dear diary" entry with its sarcasm, its bursts of emotion, its revelations of secrets, and its buildup to some climactic moment—a crisis, which at least in the 1970s version of these books could be sex, love, sibling rivalry, the ebb and flow of friendship, graduation, the very kinds of transitional moments that would go into a diary.

The challenge for publishers is that the lives those diaries record are changing; the forms in which teenagers interpret their lives are shifting. Thus the books, which both mirror and establish the ways teenagers interpret their lives, also have to change.

The two largest changes turn on the question of how to respect the borderline of mystery and privacy while also speaking to the teenagers' subterranean selves, and how to capture the voice of teenage life when the first-person form itself seems antique as a literary style and as a description of reality.

Where is the borderline of mystery today? Mass media broadcasts in prime time on national channels are obsessed with sexuality and revelations about people's private lives. The Internet allows even the most fumbling user to get to pretty salacious material in a few easy steps. What the average teenager now knows about sex is everything the rest of us once wanted to know and were afraid to ask.

Because we as a society have no sense of what cannot be said, of what does not belong in public, of what is inappropriate for general consumption, we have no clear-cut idea of what the transition of teenage entails. What new world of knowledge is the teenager entering that was not part of his or her environment years earlier?

You can see this even in consumer products. In the 1960s, mothers and daughters clashed over lipstick. Girls in their early teens wanted to wear lipstick; mothers didn't want them to advertise themselves in that way. So Maybelline invented "Fresh Face," a makeup line that allowed girls to put something on their face but hardly altered how they looked. What could possibly be the equivalent now—body piercing lite? Instead of creating products that allowed teenagers to buy their place in society—which could be called a kind of abuse—we now encourage teenagers to see themselves as twenty-somethings. There is a kids' Gap and an adult Gap, with no teenage Gap. And why would we need one? What might a teenager want to wear that would be ruled out as inappropriate?

Having grown up in broken, recombined, and even transplanted families, teenagers have already had to adjust to adults' passions and failings. As heirs of the identity politics wars and the profusion of help groups and programs of this past decade, teenagers certainly also know how many different choices of lifestyle and sexuality await them.

In one sense all of this exposure is good. It means that teenagers' private struggles over sexuality, privacy, autonomy, and intimacy are echoed in both the preoccupations of the media and an endless variety of therapeutic organizations. The space between private suffering and public knowledge has diminished. But in another way it must be daunting. The blare of publicity leaves no space for a journey that every individual must make for his or her self.

Just when teenagers are sounding out their own private depths, just when they should be feeling most clearly the fear and the attraction of transgression, they see nothing but transgression everywhere. Their own equivocations are swamped by the inevitability of sex and the evident inadequacy of adult guidance. They know too much and have too little space and respect for claiming their own knowledge in their own way.

While advertisements and broadcast media seduce teenagers, digital networks are more passive. For that very reason they are even harder to control. There is no center, only sprawl. We cannot contain what is on the Web or who has access to it. Anything a teenager seeks to find, he will discover, with no adult to monitor the process.

Here is the tricky part for publishers. To attempt to institute a reticence in our books that is absent everywhere else is a formula for disaster. One important part of our charge is to reach our readers. This is, of course, a financial imperative—we need to sell books. It is also a pact with both authors and readers: it is not fair to publish a book no one will read or be able to get through. Yet to blindly join in the flood of explicitness is, in a sense, to remove our own reason for being. What is YA fiction if it obeys exactly the same rules as adult literature?

Framing the issue this way leads to more problems but also hints at the solution. This kind of thinking defines YA literature by what it can and cannot say, rather than by its tone, its aesthetic, its ability to speak profoundly to its readers. It says that YA is a kind of halter, a restraint, on literature that, if left free, would really be adult.

If we turn this around and shift from restraints to style, aim, approach, we turn back to the challenge I described earlier: we have to make our readers feel we are familiar with the basement and that we see with their eyes just how compelling and strange it is. We have to bring them in print the feelings and sensations they are beginning to explore but have not yet quite defined. When we do, we get that classic YA reaction: "That character is just like me." In this sense, YA literature is like a splinter: when you push on the part you can see, it burns below the surface where you can't. The challenge of YA literature is not defined by censors but by the perceptual framework of readers.

Now let me add an even further wrinkle. Recently on YALSA-BK, an American Library Association listserv that deals with YA books, there was a debate about the current crop of "bleak" books. One adult, soon backed up by a teenager, put the whole issue to rest. He said, "Teenagers like bleakness; it is a popular teenage emotion." Teenagers want intense feeling, such as bleak despair, in their books. That jolt of angst, passion, fear is a good part of what characterizes many YA novels. Directness, intensity, extremity make a book feel real to these readers. They want to feel that poke, that jab, where the text hits home.

One model of YA publishing, then, would be to offer as much emotional or somatic intensity as possible. After all, even young teenagers already read Steven King or gory, semipornographic graphic novels. I'm told that YA libraries in Denmark subscribe to adult magazines like *Playboy*. But for fear of being challenged, I suspect many American librarians would too.

But then parents step in. Just this week on CCBC-net, a University of Wisconsin children's literature listserv, one librarian from a very liberal upper West Side Manhattan school reported that a parent was disturbed by our book, *Smack* (Henry Holt, 1998; Avon, 1999)—which is a story about teenagers and heroin addiction—because it did not have positive adult role models in it. In other words, that parent wanted the book itself to be a kind of adult: a rule giver who inculcated on the page the values the parent is not sure she has instilled on her own.

So here is the teenager's problem and the publisher's challenge: as society overwhelms teenagers, parents either overprotect or abandon them. To the world at large, a teenager is a potential consumer whose desires and hormones are fair game. To parents, a YA book is a manual for living, a kind of mini-Bible that serves as a babysitter for older children. What space is there between these poles?

Our books offer a place in which readers can test and explore whom they are becoming. But how do they do that? How do books give their teenage readers an opportunity to feel deeply and also to grow, to move past the sensations they already know? The most obvious answer is through identification—a book whose plot matches teen lives allows readers to feel less alone. The books that did that to a fault were the problem novels of the 1970s and 1980s. Though they may have been useful to some readers, I think books have a much grander role to play. For, at their best, books are artistic creations. And great art offers the most profound opportunity for change. Not because it teaches but because it opens up boundaries.

Here are a few examples from other media. One appeared in 1841, the other in 1913. And yet they get to the very heart of the adolescent conflicts I just described. They show that when art goes beyond identification, it can truly offer a space for transformation.

How many of you have seen the romantic ballet *Giselle*? There was a time when I went to it quite often, and just a few weeks ago I saw it again. That trip to the ballet moved me deeply. First there was the theater itself. There is something wonderful about going to a dance performance. You see the wealthy couples in tasteful, fashionable black, the Europeans adding their cultured buzz to the lobby conversations, the parents—once only mothers, now fathers as well—out with their daughters for a special evening, the dance students in standing room sneaking down for seats. The crowd makes the event feel like a ritual even before the dance begins.

As the lights darken, the anticipation begins. There is a physical edginess as people hope to be transported but hesitate, wondering if this performance will have the old magic. The familiar music, the set, the entrance of the first dancer: we are on our way.

What do we see? The first act of *Giselle* is a rather predictable story of class and romance, a nineteenth-century version of a soap opera. Hilarion, a lumbering woodsman, is in love with Giselle, a delicate village lass. A prince in disguise named Albrecht is out on his own, just ahead of a royal hunting party that includes his betrothed. In the tiny hamlet where Hilarion has just left flowers for Giselle, Albrecht has a secret life pretending to be a local boy. Albrecht is charmed by the shy, frail, and yet somehow lively girl.

His grace and spirit—and of course wonderful dancing—win Giselle's affections. And amid the bouncing, happy duets, he swears eternal love for her. Everyone warns them that this is wrong. When

Giselle finds a daisy and plucks petals to see if he loves her, the last one shows he does not. In an exchange that is about dancing, but also sex, her mother reminds Giselle that she has a weak heart and can't take the strain of all this exuberance. Her mother has a vision of the Willis, the vengeful spirits of women who die abandoned on their wedding nights. And glowering Hilarion is growing ever more jealous.

Hearing the horn of the hunting party, Albrecht scampers off to hide. He manages to stay out of the way until they leave. But Hilarion has found the sword and the hunting horn the handsome stranger tried to hide. Unable to accept the love between Albrecht and Giselle, he tries to warn off the prince. When he cannot, he blows the horn, bringing back the royal hunters.

In a short confrontation scene, Giselle realizes that her beloved already belongs to a noble lady. At that moment Giselle collapses, goes mad, and her heart breaks. Standing off to the side, Albrecht roils in his own agonies, as this pure and beautiful girl dies in front of him.

Aside from that powerful last scene, this is a formulaic act, which can still be read in a number of ways—the prince is a total cad, out for a dalliance even as he is about to be wed. Or the prince is a life-loving spirit trapped in a royal engagement he is desperate to escape; Hilarion is the loyal good Joe ignored by a girl who is dazzled by the heartless prince; or Hilarion is the jealous clod who destroys a greater love even at the cost of Giselle's life. Versions of any of these stories can be found in countless YA romances because they follow easy and quite rational plot lines.

The second act is a completely different experience. The first was a daytime story filled with flirty dances, obvious plots, and recognizable characters. Now it is night in the forest. Giselle has been buried, and first Hilarion and then Albrecht come to her grave. There they meet the Willis, the icy cold spirits Giselle's mother had envisioned. These vengeful wraiths are summoned by their queen Myrta to dance men to death.

The Willis are clad in white tutus and move in unison. Their arms wave like the tentacles of ghostly sea anemones, their lumbering feet lurch in movements that are both the absolute opposite of Giselle's airy leaps and a forecast of Graham-style modern dance. They are creatures of nightmare.

When Giselle first arrives to join them, she has a strange solo, a disturbing dervish-like twirling. One critic describes this move as "dizzying, centrifugal, it is indeed an opening out, an off-kilter uncoiling, a lightning passage into a different circle of existence."

The story in this act has been stripped to its essence: love against death. Though Hilarion is danced to death, Giselle is still human enough to help Albrecht keep dancing until cock's crow, when the Willi's power is broken. Their dancing together and in solo for each other is some of the most beautiful choreography in the romantic ballet. But the act is not merely about them. It is about unconscious and irrational drives that consume us; we do battle with them until, saved by love, we can be awakened by the dawn.

The difference between the acts is no accident. The first was written by a hack writer named Vernoy de Saint-Georges who had done many formula pieces of this sort. The second was by the arch romantic Theophile Gautier. It is exactly as if the first half of a movie were made by Ron Howard and the second by David Lynch, and yet together they made up a single experience.

The link between these two totally different scripts and temperaments, between day and night, is Giselle's mad scene. In those few minutes, she must cross from young girl to mature spirit, just as Albrecht must become the devastated lover who would risk everything to honor the very girl he has just destroyed.

The greatest Giselle of this century, Olga Spessitizva, studied people in an insane asylum to learn how to dance this section. The one film clip of her performance that exists is eerie—is it a perfect portrait of madness or a disturbing display of real derangement? Olga later spent twenty years being treated for her own breakdown.

As the ballerina Alessandra Ferri puts it, "You're almost two different women. In Act I Giselle is a young girl with a very light spirit, and then in Act II, a mature woman who understands the meaning of real love, generous love, and so has real weight in her emotions. And it's a matter of being bigger than yourself in Act II. You go beyond human feelings, and beyond the problems of human beings."

Giselle is called the "Hamlet of ballerina roles," and her mad scene is very much about the adolescent moment where every adult warning fails, and one must fight, alone, with one's own drives. To succeed is to make possible mature love, to fail is to dance yourself to death chasing phantoms or to go crazy. In that sense, the whole second act is Giselle's mad scene. It displays the struggle in her unconscious to face her rejection, her yearning, her vengeance, and her power to love. That difficult moment of passage is exactly coming-of-age.

There are two great artistic challenges in this ballet. The dancers must find a way to unite day and night, stereotypical characterizations and archetypal unconscious. But you the audience have an even greater opportunity. If you can be transported by the ballet, you can be taken into yourself, into the places within your self where these dramas are enacted. The chance Giselle offers you is not just to see a dancer realize a role but to visit yourself. In the darkened temple of the theater, the rite being enacted is your own journey from the daylight of conscious plots, calculations, and entanglements, through disorder, grief, and derangement, into the deepest, most frightening, and most redemptive drives within you.

Because it is composed of two such totally different acts, *Giselle* is a kind of symbol for what all art can do—bring together opposites in a way that forces us to examine and resolve them in ourselves.

This is the great challenge, and the great space I want to claim for the YA novel. To return to my first image, the novel is a place to experience both the first act family den and the second act adolescent basement. The novel is not just a place to see carefully laid out growth but to experience it in all of its danger and unpredictability. While everything being discussed here is important—all the ways children and teenagers and technology and society are changing or resisting change—I want us to remember that the power of great art is not defined by its time or its technology, but by how it makes connections within ourselves.

A *Time* magazine cover story a few years ago told of thirteen-and fourteen-year-olds in Salt Lake City who visit clinics wanting advice on sex techniques to enhance their enjoyment. Surely there are books that can help them. But what the best fiction can do is something else: in those novels teenagers begin to feel and explore what is going on beneath the surface of the act that has already become boring. If modern teenagers are flooded with knowledge and experience, in YA books we offer them a place to discover new meaning, new resources, new depth within themselves.

My choice of *Giselle* here is not just personal and eccentric—though I suppose it is that. The split in acts and the pressure that puts on performers and audience is similar to a technique many authors are now using in YA fiction: multiple or unreliable narrators. That is, if once the whole point of a YA novel was the first-person account of my feelings, my life, my story, now we cannot be sure whose story we are reading. We and the author may be seeing through, around, over the shoulder of the narrator. How many people reading Cormier's *Tenderness* want to yell at the girl, telling her not to fall in love with the killer?

These narrative techniques are not in themselves artistic, for you can easily have a bad novel in multiple voices. But they do draw our attention to the fact that a novel is art. Instead of pretending to be the stream of thoughts in a teenager's mind, or notes on her diary page, they are clearly the crafted creation of an author who is revealing and withholding information, and is forcing you to work with the book to sort it out.

In my own book, *Art Attack* (Clarion, 1998), I've tried a different version of multivalence. I deliberately made it interactive. And yet the centerpiece is an art work made in entirely conventional media. *Art Attack* is a history of the avant-garde. As I wrote it, I realized that I should give teenagers as many ways as possible to enter the book. So while it has a text that discusses the Armory Show or Rimbaud or Duchamp or Mahlevich, or Pollock or Hendrix or Cage, it also has a suggested soundtrack. I expect kids to blast loud music while they read it—after all, I did when I wrote it. I've made it easy, suggesting the music that fits each section. Now I've created a Web site, where they can go to see in color the art I have in black-and-white and explore further the art I discuss. I don't see multimedia as something confined to digital formats. Rather, it is an attitude, an understanding of how teenagers experience the world. I welcome my readers to take my book into their digital environment.

One of the central moments in *Art Attack* comes when I try to understand the power of *Rite of Spring*. You all know Stravinsky's music and the famous story of the scandals and fights that erupted on May 29, 1913, on the first occasion of the performance of Nijinsky's choreography. It has a lot to say about everything I've been discussing today.

Historically, the idea of an artistic avant-garde and the invention of a stage of life between childhood and adulthood came at about the same time, in Paris of the 1820s to 1840s. The contention that we needed an art that overturned all previous ideas about art and society, as well as the perception that in young adulthood people lead lives that reject parental and social values even on the road to reembracing them, arose at the same time and place. It is no coincidence

that the Parisian bohemians of those years set the model for rebellious young people that has lingered straight through to the East
Village young people of today.

But by 1913, the greatest moment of the avant-garde created a
very different link between young adulthood and rebellious art.
Stravinsky's idea for the music came from having an image of "a
solemn pagan rite: sage elders, seated in a circle, watched a young
girl dance herself to death. They were sacrificing her to propitiate
the god of spring." In his vision, there is no coming-of-age, no emer-
gence of the individual. The group rules. The young girl can only
contribute to her people by dying, by giving her blood to the passage of the seasons. Appropriately, the most controversial section of
the music is called the "dances of the adolescents."

Giselle, at the heart of the Romantic movement, is about an individual victimized by society, rising above even her own death,
doing battle with her demons, and creating an enduring image of
love both linked to and beyond the grave. By the time of the pre-
miere of *Rite of Spring*, the individual no longer matters at all. It is
as if, in some Lovecraftian sense, the Willis had taken over the first
act, and there was nothing to life but propitiating those hungry
ghouls.

Nijinsky's choreography cinched the trap even tighter. While
Stravinsky's music pummeled listeners, dominating them with the
pulse of a prehuman, subhuman savage beat, Nijinksy's angular,
off-center, inhuman choreography assaulted their eyes with the
modern world of robotic, alienated mobs. Even as the music ripped
out any hope of personal transcendence, the dance steps revealed
that human beings had become half-machines. The second force was
not redemption but mechanization. There was no space for change,
no hope that a person could make that shift from child and group
to individual and public. Art could only offer ceremonies of violence, which perfectly predicted the greater violence that erupted all
over Europe the following year.

Art captured a psychological truth that was also a historical
prophecy. That is why it was hard to watch but wonderful to think
about. If one high calling of art is to provide a place in which we
experience our own rites of passage, another is to understand how,
sometimes, that very movement is tragically impossible. The only
hope is the wrenching truth of the trap. The spate of "bleak" books
that got so much press shows that our authors are exploring this

territory too—not just books that take us through adolescence to new maturity, but books that track times and places where that passage is simply impossible.

Coming-of-age is the greatest step an individual takes, which is why the ancient Greeks made adolescence so central to their mystery cults. They understood how risky and how powerful a journey it is.

When those ancient mysteries were written down as quest stories, the hero always begins feeling vulnerable and ill equipped, not up to the task. He *is* not ready for it. Only the journey itself gives him the tools to complete it.

That is what our books can and must be: fractional and incomplete guides that speak to and for those heroes of their own journey. The books do not present answers, just space for freedom, for art, for exploration. In their tone, and their acceptance of the reader, they allow for what lurks and looms in the basement. They neither force the reader to see too much nor hide anything. This is a supremely difficult challenge, and a wonderful one.

If I cannot give you a clear map of how YA literature will evolve, I hope I have given you a sense of what is at stake in these books, why they matter, and why they deserve our honor and our respect.

9

✛

What Is Real about Realism?
All the Wrong Questions
about YA Literature

> While I was working on *Art Attack*, I kept thinking about how
> art, teenage, and YA literature connect, or fail to do so. This
> speech deals with the two main places where the literature for
> teenagers—at least as it had been defined by reviewers, teach-
> ers, parents, and librarians—splits off from the main art trends
> of our time: the insistence on "realism" and the pressure for
> "moral messages." Since I deal with related issues in some of
> the other chapters in this book, I've trimmed this to highlight
> those two issues—realism and moralism.

I'm here to tell you that the association of teenage fiction with realism, and the effort to impose a moral mission on books—while a
perverse kind of bow to the power of art—actually ensure that
young readers are denied contact with the great art of their time.
These beliefs punish the authors who can best bridge the gap between adult and teenage; they trap young adult readers in a ghetto
of the tame, the limited, the second-rate, the obvious, the unambi-
tious.

If you had to pick one word that is used over and over again to
characterize YA fiction, it would be "realistic." And if you had to

pick a single question that is asked just as frequently about those "realistic" novels, it would be "What message do they have for our impressionable, at-risk, in-need-of-role-models, in-need-of-self-esteem teenagers?"

No one seems to notice that these two are opposites. Realism is not concerned with morality; it is about verisimilitude. Morality is not interested in fidelity to experience but in shaping beliefs or behaviors. Much realism is amoral or antimoral. Some of the best-known didactic writing comes in the form of fables. But even if we leave that inherent contradiction aside, there is a fundamental problem with this whole construction of the teenage reading experience.

Adolescence is one of the most difficult and important periods in life. It is when we enter the territory of the forbidden and, through doing that, master ourselves in a fashion that allows us to become adult—on psychological, social, and civic levels. But it is equally true in terms of art. We cannot confine art to safe precincts if we want it to work its magic.

An artist is a shaman. All of us tell stories to ourselves every day, but we don't call them stories. We call them anger ("That idiot, he . . ."), lust ("She's so beautiful I wish I . . ."), regret ("I wish I hadn't . . ."), hope ("If only I could . . ."). We replay these tapes to ourselves all day long. The artist can take those half-articulated fractions and fragments and give them form. We feel artists to be magicians because they seem to know our thoughts and have the ability to show them to us. An artist builds an image in front of our eyes that echoes within the deepest recesses where our very self is formed.

Teenagers are struggling with profound conflicts, all the deeper because they do not recognize yet what they are facing. The artist takes the clay, the dross that all of us are surrounded with, and fashions it into something that seems to have not only life but our own lives in it. We yearn for artists to give us more truth, to show us ourselves so that we know who we are.

This should be a perfect fit—the teenager is in the crucial stage of forming a self, and the artist has the tools to reflect and give form to exactly that process. This is the precise moment at which critics of YA literature falter. They see the kids filled with needs and conflicts; they see the authors poised to write great narratives of the soul's journey, and they try to match them up.

It doesn't work that way.

Neither art nor adolescence can be tamed that easily. This presents a problem, to be sure, but it is also very exciting. When we can see how the two actually connect, it is one of the most fertile, dynamic, and important links we can ever make in our lives. When teenagers truly experience a piece of art that moves them, that reaches them, it can affect them as at no other age. We have to open the gates to make that experience possible in every way we can.

The first problem is defining what is real. We adults live in a relatively continuous narrative: we know from day to day what our obligations and responsibilities will be. A balanced checkbook, a promotion, a child safely into the right school is a happy ending we believe in. Yet for nearly two hundred years, artists have sought to disrupt that story of bourgeois progress and contentment. To the great artists of our time, realism in art has meant matching the disruptions, the discontinuities, the overlapping layers of meaning that are true of both our subconscious realities and the actual facts of our divided societies. The "realism" of moral messages and happy endings is precisely what artists have told us is unreal, a saccharine coating meant to disguise these unsettling truths.

While teenagers also have markers in their lives, they are far less sure which narrative will dominate: their parents' beliefs, their friends' attitudes, their heroes' examples. These simultaneous, overlapping, and competing narratives are very much like what artists tell us is "real" reality. Think of a teenager in her room reading some solid text with all of the right messages for school, listening to the music she likes (which may be full of riot and rebellion), surfing Web sites that have every possible point of view, doing instant messaging with friends who are equally surrounded by congeries of competing voices, fending off the sober appeals of her parents just outside the door, and carrying on endless phone conversations with folks who don't happen to be online. What is it about a normal narrative in a so-called realistic novel that in any way resembles this cacophony, this collage, of differing voices?

As soon as we give up our demand that art for teenagers be characterized by phony realism, we can begin to reconnect teenagers with the art and the experience of their time. Here YA authors are taking the lead. At one time, in the interest of mimicking the tone of a diary or interior monologue, the YA novel had to be in the first person. It was the sequence of thoughts of the main character. Now authors are writing books with many competing voices, each trying to tell their own story. This is not only like the experience of the teenager I just described, but it is precisely similar to the experience of a child whose parents have divorced or remarried into new blended families. That child knows in his bones that stories have many different narratives, many different truths, depending on your point of view.

In *Whirligig* by Paul Fleischman (Holt, 1998), this is taken even further. The voices are not sequential, and the form of the book is the story of the book—the idea that there are hidden connections between things and that we can never fully know the consequences of our acts. Asked whether he had any problems with this odd structure, a thirteen-year-old answered, "Well, maybe it was too simple."

Even as we try to confine fiction for teenagers to "realism," they are living in a point-and-click world in which reality is multiple choice and digital connections.

I know that many teenagers do, though, prefer something they call realism. When I speak with them, the word that comes up most often as praise is "real." "This book felt real to me."

Figuring out what they mean by that will get to my second main point about art and teenage. I think they mean "real" as opposed to sugar coated. That is, their task as teenagers is to leave childhood behind. As they enter the basement of their own sexuality, their perceptions are sharpened. Not only are they aware of themselves in new ways, but they see others differently. They feel desire, and that they are desired.

A book that seems to take this world for granted is a great relief to them. It is in that sense real. But that realistic quality has nothing to do with realism in the limited sense that parents and critics use. It is real because it goes beneath the surface, because it tells a truth people don't want to see, because it doesn't settle, it provokes.

All of these are precisely the qualities of great art. So even as I urge you to expose teenagers to the fiction of their own time, the young adult fiction that uses the forms and challenges of life in the multichanneled, disjunctive, digital world as its base, I also think it is crucial that they be exposed to works such as *Romeo and Juliet*, the ballet *Giselle*, Magritte's *The Treason of Images*, Joyce's *Portrait of the Artist as a Young Man* (B. W. Huebsch, 1916).

If we judged any of those art works by the supposed moral standard I mentioned at first, they would fail—one shows a teenage suicide pact, another is the tale of a girl jilted by a jerky prince, who kills herself (or dies of a broken heart), the third is an image that makes you question all images, and the last anguishes over a crisis of faith.

If we were to measure any of them by their "message," they would be found wanting. But if, instead of judging an artwork by our blinkered, limited, pedestrian effort to assign it a morality, we looked at how it opened us up, how it made us see ourselves in new ways, how it added depth to our lives, then all are triumphs.

Those art works take you to places in yourself you did not even know existed. I can think of no greater service to teenagers than to give them the experience of delving deeper into themselves so that they find resources that they did not know they possessed.

Our duty as adults is to keep leading them toward works that have that magical capacity to take them into the depths that they are only beginning to recognize are theirs. The works that really do this are works that we cannot control. We are handing over unstable works of art to unstable kids. That is a risk, but a worthy one.

So here's the choice: predigested morals and fake realities that readers will soon see through or books that take readers to discover new realities in themselves and derive their moral quality from their unpredictable depths. One is safe and guaranteed to make readers dislike reading and distrust adults. The other entrusts in readers the capacity to grow past us. I say it is no choice. We owe the artists of our time the chance to speak to their coming audience, and we owe those readers the gift of art.

So next time anyone asks you, "Is it realistic" or "What message does it send," answer, "No, it is profound, and because of that the teenagers who read it will find their own messages, which they will receive in their own ways."

10

✤

The Power of Words

This is a speech that I gave to New York YA librarians. It is specifically about censorship, but I used that frame as an opportunity to look at what words offer to readers—their danger and their power. In that sense it relies on and extends the arguments I make about art, and what art can do with and for teenagers, in other chapters.

I want to talk to you today about words, about language, about story. Words are what get us into trouble, from when we are kids going through that cursing phase to when we are adults and people curse back at us. Before we can even begin to think about which books should be published or shelved in a library, we have to think about words, and language, and story.

Passover is coming up, and all of you who have been to seders know that you shake off little droplets of wine as you count off each of the ten plagues. Having been to many speeches in my day, I know that, as a listener, it is a life saver to know where the speaker is, how far along, how much is left to go. So, as we do at a seder, I am going to number off and give you the six ways words work. That way, as each topic comes and goes, you can mentally shake off a droplet and see how long it is until you can stand up and stretch. My six themes are identification, speech, invention, responsibility, truth, and the endless conversation.

Words are some of the most fragile and yet most potent tools we use everyday. Certainly they are fragile. They are helpless against money, physical force, disease, or accidents of nature. But they may be our most powerful creation, for words stand between our experiences, our ever so frail, human, and trivial lives, and other people. Words are some of the first gifts we give to children. In books for young people we use words to tell stories, and yet the words themselves are a continual enhancement and enlargement of the reader's world. Words, you might say, bridge the human and the divine.

Don't worry, this is not a sermon. As my fiancée and I planned our wedding, one thing I insisted on was a rabbi who didn't take himself too seriously. But there are some things the Bible puts very well, and one of them is the power of words. Of course, the Gospel according to John begins, "In the beginning was the word." But that is a particular meaning of word, Logos.

What Genesis says about words is easier to follow. Genesis is about beginnings, and in the third verse of the first chapter, as creation takes form, we see that "God said, let there be light, and there was light." Naming light made light be. That is exactly what happens to us every day, and to a child as he or she grows. As we name, and define, and give shape and words to our experiences, they separate out from the formless and become distinct. They become something that we can understand and share.

In the beginning there is the word because it is the word that makes a beginning. The African American poet James Weldon Johnson tells of the moment where God said,

> "I'm lonely—
> I'll make me a world."

Words begin to articulate what we feel and what we think—our loneliness and our desire to make a world. They are the atom-thin shell of description we place around what takes place inside us so that these things have names, so that they can be shared, so that they can be understood. This is most evident in poetry, where an artist takes a feeling, an experience, no matter how fleeting or devastating, and finds the words to give it eternal shape.

Because we sense the power of words, we care a great deal about how they are used in books for children. But our caring is not the same as understanding how books, words, and children are actually linked.

Just last weekend I was out in Wisconsin, at the Cooperative Children's Book Center conference on "Radical Change in Children's Books," where the biggest fight was about words. Some claimed that we had better police the words in children's books very carefully, so that no one, especially no one from a group that has been oppressed or victimized, should be offended. Others argued that we have to leave room for an author to play with words, and that once we admit the principle of policing, we have to be as careful of the sensitivities of those who see Satan in Halloween as those who feel offended by the large black woman in Bruce Brooks's novel, *Everywhere* (Harper, 1990).

What is the real power of words, and what is the real threat? Almost all of the censorship cases boil down to that question. How can words open children to life, to knowledge, to understanding, and how can words harm them?

The most obvious way that language and story can help a child is through identification. The child sees himself in a character or situation and begins to understand a bit more about life and his own inner self. The story is a rung the child can grasp onto in the climb toward being an adult.

The great achievement of the last thirty years in children's books is how many more of these handholds we have extended to children. The fact that I can have an imprint devoted to international and multicultural coming-of-age books is an extraordinary and quite recent development. For this to work, I must have two difficult things: enough authors writing those books, and enough people who want to read them. Fortunately, every day when I pick up the paper, I see a potential new EDGE book: whether it is in the lives of immigrant teenagers or in the mestizo heritage Americans are just starting to acknowledge or in the stereotypes that still fill our ads and political campaigns (all of these are the subjects of upcoming books).

Actually, the easiest way to recognize how much children's books have changed is by seeing what we don't have. This is my quick list; tell me if I've missed something: we are low on multicultural board books, we have far more folktales than contemporary stories about kids in other cultures, we don't publish enough about the Indian subcontinent, we have barely begun to explore the world of Islam, America's Spanish heritage is largely invisible, and religious Americans are wildly underrepresented in our fiction and history books. Can you name another big lack?

These are significant gaps. But to come up with them, we have to pause a moment and think of a person or experience missing from our shelves. Not so long ago, we had to pause a good long time to think of any nonwhite person or experience that was included at all or was not treated in a patronizing fashion. The last big conflict I had about a multicultural book shows how far we have extended the borderlines of identification in books for younger readers.

Last year, Jacqueline Woodson was working on an anthology for us called *A Way Out of No Way* (Holt, 1996). This collection was her personal gathering of writings by black authors about coming-of-age. She wanted to include a poem by the controversial poet Sapphire that described "wilding"—the rape and attempted murder of a female jogger in Central Park—from the point of view of one of the kids who did it. In the end, she decided not to include the poem. She realized it would have required too much explanation to show how Sapphire's chant revealed and explained but did not condone the boy's actions.

If the outer edge of stories that we can share with young people is defined by the monologue of a rapist and attempted murderer, we have plenty of room to roam. Not too many kids are prevented by this hesitation from finding themselves, their own stories, in print.

Even as we include more and more kinds of people in books for younger readers, we have also expanded the range of families and feelings that appear in print. Just this spring, for example, three new books have come out that explore ambiguities in a teenager's sexuality. Barbara Wersba's *Whistle Me Home* (Holt, 1997), like M. E. Kerr's *Hello, I Lied* (HarperCollins, 1997), deals with the complexities of relationship between a gay guy and a straight girl, while Rodger Larson's *What I Know Now* (Holt, 1997, is about a fourteen-year-old boy who is in love with a man but also fantasizes about women. And this fall, Jacqueline Woodson is publishing a book called *The House You Pass on the Way* (Bantam, 1997), which explores similar ambiguities that cross lines of both gender and race.

Instead of merely telling stories whose punch line is that a character is different and that is okay, we are now getting books in which a character is ambiguous, sorting out a mixed identity, and that is okay too. Handholds don't have to be single choices; books can offer identification even to a state of uncertainty—*especially* to a state of uncertainty.

This ever-expanding diversity of stories is something we can all feel proud of. It shows that we all see the power of language to expand a child's world through identification. But it is exactly this property of words to mimic a child's world that causes trouble.

See, now we are all feeling kind of good about ourselves. We've gotten through the first drop of wine pretty painlessly and we can pat ourselves on the back for our shelves, now bulging with multicultural tales. But I am about to pull the rug out from underneath us. For just as we reach the place where we think we can feel complacent, we open ourselves to attack.

If we are pleased that kids can now find a wide range of characters to identify with in books, and if we think that this can open up their lives to new possibilities, we are accepting the very argument of those who want to censor books. If kids are likely to identify with characters and thus become those characters, we had better be very careful about which characters appear in books.

When people seek to limit what kids read, they too have a sense of the power of words, even of their magic. But the magic they believe in is a kind of voodoo. They think that if you exclude terms and experiences from books, you will eliminate them from a child's life. Like sticking pins in a doll to hurt a rival, if you ban the book, you ban the thing. They also believe in the "positive" form of this: if you give kids only "good" books, well-chosen exemplars of all of the right behaviors and attitudes, kids will come to resemble those models. Either by banning "negative" ideas, experiences, and characters or by featuring "positive" ones, you use words and the power of identification to shape a child's future.

It is easy to sneer at this point of view, although that also gets a bit uncomfortable when the argument shifts from censorship on behalf of fundamentalists to censorship on behalf of women or minority groups. But beating behind all of these efforts to control books is actually something quite interesting. I think all of these censors are mistaking words on pages for words spoken. They are treating books as speech. Censors see books as acting in loco parentis, as speaking to children and telling them how to behave. Parents and critics—from the left or the right—who seek to ban books are afraid of that voice. They fear that the author might twist, molest, subvert their child when the author has him alone, credulous, and vulnerable. When a parent asks, "What kind of message are you sending to my child?" this is what she means. That mother is asking a book to act as a parable, an oral story.

Much of our literature comes from an oral tradition. Certainly this is true of folktales, but also Homer, the Norse sagas, modern African writers like Chinua Achebe, and so on. One crucial difference between an oral literature and a written one is that the first is spoken and is shared by a community; the second is read and is absorbed by an individual. Oral literature is public: the shaman, griot, or grandmother leads and guides. Her words carry the burden of everyone's shared traditions; not only do they speak *to* the listener, they speak *for* the group. Sitting in a circle, we are drawn together by hearing the same story. Storytelling, no matter how entertaining, is generally a sacred and profoundly pedagogical act.

N. Scott Momaday spells all of this out:

> "At the heart of the American Indian oral tradition is a deep and unconditional belief in the efficacy of language. Words are intrinsically powerful. They are magical. By means of words can one bring about physical change in the universe." This power poses great dangers to the speaker. "When one ventures to speak . . . he assumes great risks and responsibilities. . . . To be careless in the presence of words, on the inside of language, is to violate a fundamental morality." (*The Man Made of Words*, St. Martin's, 1997)

So here we have the Native American storyteller feeling the potential magic of his words, gathering himself in stoic silence to speak deliberately, to speak well. The weight of his power, and of his community's needs, and of his ancestors, rests on his shoulders. This is how censors would have authors comport themselves, as the storytellers guiding our community. But books, words in print, do not work the same way as oral stories.

A child reading, I would argue, is not the passive recipient of wisdom our critics see. Instead she herself is much more like the storyteller. She is constantly taking stories told to her and reshaping them in her mind. A book is more private and more complex than an oral story. The meaning is much less stable. The reader is alone with words, free to play with them in her mind. Stories change with tellers; books change with readers.

Neither does a child become gay because he reads a book about a gay character, nor does he become good because he reads a moralistic fable. As Bruce Brooks put it in *Boys Will Be* (Holt, 1993),

> Every bully who has appeared in print or on the screen . . . shows himself to be a totally repulsive, ugly-hearted, morally indecent, stupid

fiend. But who have we convinced? . . . Either the children we should be reaching are not paying attention, or—most likely—they are laughing raucously (as they steal candy from the wee Nice Child sitting to their left). (p. 49)

YA novels and Sunday school homilies blend into the churning already taking place inside the boy who reads them. The child does not become the story; the story becomes the child.

It is this process of assimilation and reinvention, of re-creation, that every artist does all of the time. The more exposure young readers have to books in which they feel this process of invention taking place—this ferment of image, fantasy, narrative, humor, love—the more books enhance and empower the process of creation taking place in the child.

We owe it to ourselves to have open libraries because we honor the power of words, which is the power of invention in the hands and heart and mind of a child.

That sounds quite grand, but I don't mean it as airy rhetoric. A literature professor named Mark Turner took off some years to study neurology so that he could understand how the brain processes stories. In his book, *The Literary Mind* (Oxford University Press, 1996), he argues that storytelling is not just something that happens in books or on TV. It is what all of us do all of the time. It is fundamental to what makes us human.

Turner argues that inside our brains, inside every sentence we say to ourselves, is a little story. Think of this scenario: a batter hits a lazy fly ball just between center and left. Allison and Jennifer both have an easy shot at it. What does one call out to the other? "I've got it." And when the teacher explains a difficult problem, and Michael suddenly figures it out, what does he say?, "I get it." And when Rasheed applies for college, his friends will say, "Did you get in?"

Turner says that all of these conjugations of "get" hearken back to that first moment when a baby grabs an object. The baby literally "gets" it. Storytelling begins with physical action: I see it, I touch it, I lose it, I find it. Every romance, every novel, every chase and adventure flick is right there, as a baby reaches out at a ball, a mobile, his mother's breast. All of adult life consists of learning new ways to map meanings onto those basic stories, learning new ways to expand the story of "I see, I touch, I lose, I find" to explain the changing nature of our lives.

This is like a muscle that we need to keep exercising. By reading many stories, we keep seeing these most fundamental experiences that are deep inside all of us, in new ways. As we read, we map experience onto parable, onto fable, onto metaphor, onto epic. Story is not just about identification; it is about creating who we are. We need open libraries so that children can keep exercising that capacity over and over. Not just, "I see myself," but "I see *a* self"; I see how it is possible to imagine the world.

The promise of interactive media has always been that it will simulate on screen, and thus stimulate in a child's mind, exactly this process of making links and connections. This is both true and false. The visual/somatic satisfaction of pointing, clicking, and going somewhere else leads to new information, new sources, new images. It makes it easier for a child to step outside of his world. But the technology is slow; it never quite delivers the full range of sound and sight it promises. And there is a fundamental difference between what happens out there on a screen and what takes place in here, inside your mind.

What we find on the Web is what others have placed there for their own reasons. Finding a site only enhances my life if I can understand and evaluate what is on it. The Web does not inherently lead me further into myself, and thus into a more complex and subtle relationship with the world. Rather it can leave me stranded in a land of electronic wallpaper. The Web offers information and communication, not knowledge. At this point it remains what it was initially designed to be: one great electronic footnote to the oral and print narratives around which we build our lives.

So far we have viewed the challenge of words from the point of view of the reader. But now, having covered identification, speech, and invention, we have reached the fourth drop of wine, our responsibility to authors. Let me give you another example from, selfishly enough, another book we are going to publish soon. This is *The Beautiful Days of My Youth* (Holt, 1997) a diary that Ana Novac kept as a fourteen-year-old while she was in Auschwitz and Plazow. This was a very interesting book to work on, for many reasons.

When it was published in France, where Ana lives, the readers of *Elle* voted it the best adult book of 1993. But when I read it, I worried it was too good. Could a fourteen-year-old really have written this, especially in Auschwitz? So I showed it to scholars, got their opinions, and sent the questions they raised to Ana.

She told us that for a year before being sent off she had been in a sanitarium, where she lived in her diary. She lived for words. And so when she arrived in the camp, her only necessity, her lifeblood, was writing, with pencil stubs, on scraps of paper.

Here is something she wrote: " 'Torment.' 'Burning Sun.' The fact that I used those words before today seems unbelievable, frivolous. If wasted words had a voice, what a fuss they'd make. 'What right do you have to use us lightly?' Here we earn the 'right' to one or two every day. And now I have a right to 'torment' and 'burning sun.' "

Ana's right to her words is her experience. She earned that right in pain, and she has to speak, she has to be heard, or that pain is lost, meaningless. She says, "I'm not writing for myself, that goes without saying. I hope that these notes will be part of the evidence, on the day of reckoning!" And so they have become. This too is why words matter so much. They are the record of what we would otherwise lose. They speak for what others wish to silence. In protecting words you honor the experiences that led to their creation.

We have a responsibility to words, to the experiences that they record, to the anguish etched in them. We cannot treat them lightly. When we consider a book, we see it as an object with a price tag—whether that be the cost in dollars or in the mental and emotional effort it takes to defend them. But a book is not just that, it is hewn out of a life. The stories in books make the connection between the unique, the personal, the quixotic, and the general, the agreed-upon, the world as we know it.

To the Norse peoples, there was a bridge between hel, the land of the dead, and the human world, guarded by a god whose ears were so sensitive he could hear grass growing. Words are that bridge and you are its guardians. You have the responsibility of protecting people's life stories.

But responsibility cuts two ways. You as librarians, and we as editors, have a second function in guarding the bridge of words, not merely to protect it from attack but to prevent its being taken over and used to bring harm.

This is a very difficult role to puzzle out. An important achievement of this century is that we have accepted, made normal, the impulses of our subconscious. Sexuality, violence, hatred, self-hatred are all part of our daily vocabulary, our common culture. This has freed us in many ways. Personally, it has allowed us to explore and understand aspects of ourselves that we would have hidden in earlier times: complex sexual urges; violent, destructive, and self-destructive impulses; yearnings to step out of proscribed patterns. Socially, it has made it much easier to bring to light abuses that families once sought desperately to hide. There is no love that cannot speak its name, no madwoman in the attic. We can say what once could never be said.

But what, then, should not be said, especially in works for children? Where does the power of words become the abuse of trust? I think there are two different answers to this, for you and for me. For me, abuse comes in two ways, for which I have two remedies. It can come in topics I find inappropriate to my readers or in the ways the author treats the topics he or she discusses, whatever they may be. My remedy is either to make changes in the text or to reject the book. The ultimate question I must answer is not "should this book come before the public?" but "should it, in this form, come to the public from me?"

You don't have the freedom to be that individualistic, that eccentric. You have a more difficult and more general question to answer: should the public see it at all? Though we have different challenges, there may be a common standard we can employ, and it gets back to words and the space they leave for invention.

Does this book respect the reader as a person? Does it respect that person's privacy as well as that person's hidden yearnings longing for exposure? Does it, ultimately, make it more possible for that person to take his or her own fragile, fleeting, hesitant experience and speak it? Or does it flatten that person into a counter, a body, a statistic waiting to be used? Is the book a propagandistic, prurient assault, or a poetic, personal creation? Does it treat the reader as a person or as an object?

Let me give you yet another personal example of how this difficult standard works on my side of the table. Last year I began working on one of the books I mentioned before, a first novel called *What I Know Now*. Rodger Larson's book is about a dreamy fourteen-year-old boy named Dave in California in 1957 whose family breaks up. His mother hires a gardener to help fix up the house, and soon Dave falls in love with Gene—who is both a better dad than his dad and a handsome, strong young man. Rodger had written the whole book, and though there were strong scenes throughout, the ending was clearly wrong.

After one particularly hot day of working, Dave and Gene went swimming naked in an irrigation ditch, along with some Mexican farm workers. The men compared their circumcised and uncircumcised anatomies and Dave learned a lesson about folks being all the same. Then, in a rapid windup, Gene was beaten in an anachronistic gay bashing scene and the book stumbled to its philosophical ending.

These scenes were false. They were not true to Dave, to Gene, to the rest of the sensitive and complex book. I realized that Rodger had been afraid to follow where his own book was taking him: that Dave would be aroused by swimming with Gene and that—on some level at least—Gene would know this. Rodger was afraid of the implication both of Dave's desire and of Gene's irresponsibility. But when he changed the scene, cut the UNESCO circumcision-comparison moment and the equally didactic gay bashing, and followed the characters' feelings, the scene made sense, and the ending of the book became obvious.

He had already written a next scene in which Gene said, somewhat ominously, "There's a lot you don't know about me." Rodger intuitively knew that Gene had to back away because he was scared of himself, that he was aware of toying with someone he cared about. Once that became more evident in the swimming scene, the conclusion of the novel was staring at us. Emotional honesty and aesthetic achievement arrived together. The new ending offered the same kind of subtle and subliminal truth as the rest of the book.

So this is the tricky problem. Rodger had avoided his own truth because of fears of its implications. But that made a worse book, a book that would have less to say, that would not as fully honor its readers, that would not as truly respect their complexity. All of the reviews, including Roger Sutton in the *Horn Book* and a starred review in Kirkus, have singled out the book's truth, its fidelity to the powerful but uncertain urgencies of coming of age. So all I can say to you is to look for the glint of truth, in all of its ambiguity. In books that have it, you will find books that respect readers.

The kind of truth I look for in literature is about gaps, absences, places where the world opens up for a child to recreate it in his or her own way. Just as I was working on this speech, I was looking at a collection of Native American trickster tales. In story after story Coyote is smart, quick, untrustworthy, and vulnerable to attack. If you read enough of these tales, he often gets burned, beaten, even killed—though he usually wins out in the end. Coyote is a creature who slips between the cracks in the world and is clever enough to remake it.

Coyote, then, is the very emblem of truth in kids' books. He speaks for that spirit of middle grade through high school kids who are coming into a world of massive yet stupid gods. What I respect in an artist is that Coyote-like temperament. You see that in their humor, passion, anger, sweetness. They go their own way in the world, and that is how they most inspire kids to grow.

The lever through which an artist can move the world is his or her integrity, his or her individual point of view. It is not subject or even style. It is integrity. You can write a YA novel about being gay, or about incest, or about the evils of capitalism that is entirely conventional. Why? Because you have written programmatic, stamped-out, flat literature. You may have the skill or craft of the good propagandist, the well-schooled hack, but you will not have depth. And depth is where true literature lies.

This also means that a totally reassuring book about mom and dad and sis can be quite radical, if embedded in the line-by-line writing, the construction of sentences, is a unique sensibility that says: pay attention to how I see the world; it matters, my view, what I project on the blank page. The most important thing we as editors, educators, librarians, and reviewers can do is to make space for that blank page, for that place where an individual temperament expresses itself, that gap between worlds that Coyote or Blue Jay or Grandmother Spider slides through.

I had to work with Rodger to get the story right. That helped resolve my guarding-the-bridge conflicts. But what about you? Which books, however good, are worth protecting? To answer that I can only offer an extended quotation from the person who most recently had most cause to think about censorship: Salman Rushdie. Rushdie grew up in a home where books were so valued that if one fell on the floor, you kissed it before you returned it to its place. This is what he has to say about books, their power, and what they offer us:

> Imagine this. You wake up one morning and find yourself in a large, rambling house. As you wander through it you realize it is so enormous that you will never know it all. In the house are people you know, family members, friends, lovers, colleagues; also many strangers. . . . This house is not what you'd have chosen, it's in fairly bad condition, the corridors are often full of bullies, but it will have to do.

Then one day you enter an unimportant-looking little room. The room is empty, but there are voices in it, voices that seem to be whispering just to you. You recognize some of the voices, others are completely unknown to you. The voices are talking about the house, about everyone in it, about everything that is happening and has happened and should happen. Some of them speak exclusively in obscenities. Some are bitchy. Some are loving. Some are funny. Some are sad. The most interesting voices are all these things at once. You begin to go to the room more and more often. Slowly you learn that most of the people in the house use such rooms sometimes. Yet the rooms are all discretely positioned and unimportant-looking.

Now imagine that you wake up one morning and you are still in the large house, but all the voice rooms have disappeared. It is as if they have been wiped out. Now there is nowhere in the whole house where you can go to hear voices talking about everything in every possible way. There is nowhere to go for the voices that can be funny one minute and sad the next, that can sound raucous and melodic in the course of the same sentence. Now you remember: there is no way out of this house. Now this fact begins to seem unbearable. You look into the eyes of the people in the corridors—family, friends, colleagues, strangers, bullies, priests. You see the same thing in everybody's eyes. *How do we get out of here*? It becomes clear that the house is a prison. People begin to scream, and pound the walls. Men arrive with guns. The house begins to shake. You do not wake up. You are already awake. (*Imaginary Homelands*, p. 428)

Rushdie ends with this conclusion: "Literature is the one place in society where, within the secrecy of our own heads, we can hear *voices talking about everything in every possible way.*"

If that house he is talking about is not a prison, if those rooms are kept open, then it is a library, the place where all of these voices speak.

What I want to charge you with today is a sense of the immense power of those books on your shelves. They have the power of identification and of innovation; they bear the weight of people's life stories; they are full of gaps, and absences, slippery places where readers can slide through into their own depths; and they are part of the infinite conversation that makes us human.

If God spoke and said he was lonely so he'd build a world, let us answer that we're lonely too, so we'll build buildings full of words. And we, you, will treat them as the great treasure they are, the bridge from one loneliness to Another.

11

✛

The Myths of Teenage

This piece comes from a conference on teenagers and reading that I organized at the New York University Publishing Program in March 1999. The fact that we were able to hold such a meeting with a large, paying audience and that we could find many speakers willing to travel across the country to discuss the subject showed how far we have come. Teenagers are clearly back on the map. Figuring out what they are reading and trying to match them up with books matters to librarians, book and magazine editors, authors, and critics. My introduction aimed at finding the source of our ignorance in our own adult assumptions. I give a broad overview of the rest of the day's events at the end of this chapter.

Greetings. My name is Marc Aronson. As some of you know, I edit books, many of them aimed at teenagers. For years, doing that required a kind of faith—faith that there were authors who would want to write superb books in a genre that is often ignored or held in contempt; faith that there were readers eager for those books; faith, ultimately that books could matter in the lives of young people who have grown up with every other form of media and entertainment. I'll be your host today. And this conference is a sign that many people share my blind and willful trust in both reading and adolescents.

This conference was born out of a myth, not Chronos or Osiris or

Yggdrasil, but the modern and pernicious kind of myth that shapes our lives. Not very long ago, I'd atttend the meetings in which new book acquisitions were approved by the higher-ups, and I'd hear: "Blacks don't buy books." This was astonishing. Important people running large companies were living in a myth-suffused haze in which prejudice defined perception. Hearing something like that stops you in your tracks. It is so far from reality, yet it is expressed with complete authority. And these beliefs matter. For a time, it was difficult to publish black-oriented books because of this reigning faith.

Luckily, the market, the talent of black authors and artists, the active interest of critics and librarians, as well as conscientious efforts by editors such as Phyllis Fogelman, did what I, as a powerless junior editor, was unable to do: show that the beliefs that were governing publishing and were deemed market facts were nothing but an amalgam of prejudice, fear, laziness, and stories. In other words, a myth was masquerading as a truth, and out of inertia, bias, or fear, people bowed down to it.

Today, there are myths in publishing that are just as powerful and just as pernicious, and that is why we are here. I believe that our state of knowledge about teenagers, and in particular about teenagers and reading, is equivalent to what it was when recycled prejudice about black Americans passed as market truth, and I can prove it.

Here are the statements that are most commonly made about teenagers and reading: "Teenagers don't read" (sometimes modified to "teenage boys don't read"). "Teenagers over the age of fourteen, fifteen, sixteen" (fill in the blanks) "only read adult books," sometimes modified to "at least that's what I remember." Finally, "teenagers have too much to read for school; they have no time for recreational reading."

Listening to those three beliefs spoken out loud, you can't help seeing that they are contradictory. If you aren't reading, you certainly are not reading adult books. If you are reading adult books, it means you do have time after your homework is done. Contradictory as these statements are, they have provided a kind of comfort to publishers, booksellers, and library directors. They were a built-in set of excuses for not trying, for making no effort to reach teenage readers, especially older ones.

There may be some level of fact behind each one of these beliefs.

That is one thing I hope we discuss and determine today. But that doesn't resolve the contradiction. The problem isn't that each statement may be partially true. It is, rather, that they are each stated as if they were total and final truths that set standards for how and what we should publish. In other words, whatever their origin in life, they have become sacred myths.

Why is that? Why do we treat these myths as truths? I think it is because they fit certain adult needs and attitudes. The first myth—"teenagers, especially boys, don't read"—is a mixture of fear and nostalgia. The fear is that teenagers will not replicate us, will not carry on the values and traditions we care about. It is an expression of our fear that we haven't done our job well. We haven't made reading central, so we don't trust that the next generation will treasure it.

I say that because a second's thought will show that teenagers, especially boys, read a great deal. How could they install new programs, pass driving tests, select precisely the right clothing and look, know all about their favorite teams, stars, musicians, and even writers if they weren't constantly reading?

That is where nostalgia comes in. When we say reading, we mean literary fiction. "Teenagers aren't reading," then, really means, "I fear that even though I want to believe I loved great novels when I was young, I haven't loved them enough as an adult to pass that along to the young. Perhaps my regrets about not having read more will come back to haunt me in the form of a generation that doesn't read literary fiction. If only teenagers read more, I'd feel better about reading less."

Myth one shows nostalgia and anxiety about our heritage. Myth two, that teenagers over a certain age only read adult books, is a different kind of projection. It is another combination of fear and hope.

The greatest anxiety teenagers inspire in adults is a fear of loss of control. This almost-child is being let out into the world just at the point where he or she could do or suffer real damage. Saying they only read adult books is another kind of resignation: we can't hold them back, we are intimidated by them. They know too much already. Adult books, in that sense, stand for the whole adult world of experience, of media, of temptation that parents turn their teenagers over to.

It is true that teenagers are ever more sophisticated, which must be daunting to parents. Parents no longer have a clear line over what is or is not appropriate for a teenager who has certainly had sex education in school as well as on TV, through friends, family, and Calvin Klein ads. But this sense of being defeated by, and resigning in the face of, teenagers' difficult urges is nothing new. Shakespeare put it very well in *The Winter's Tale*, a play all about the bonds of love: "I would there were no age between ten and three and twenty, or that youth would sleep out the rest, for there is nothing in between but getting wenches with child, wronging the ancientry, stealing, [and] fighting."

Like Shakespeare, parents wish young people would sleep from before puberty until after college, when they can earn a living and help pay off debts. If reading adult books hurries along that happy day, all the better.

Yet there is also a twist here. A parent might fight over, not merely accept, a teenager's interest in other purely adult forms of media. But not with books. Why? Because books still carry a kind of cultural authority and hope. Parents are proud to report that their children are reading adult books, while few would boast that their cute kids are sneaking into X-rated movies. If the way in which teenagers are taking in the adult world, the formerly forbidden world of sexuality, deviance, evil, or strange beliefs, is through adult books, at least there is a kind of maturity in that. By mentally passing the teenager over to adult books and simultaneously agreeing to ignore him or her, the parent both gives up and hopes that the young person is moving on. If teenagers are reading explicit books, at least they are adult explicit books.

In a singular cocktail of resignation and magical thinking, adults entrust their silent, uncommunicative, dangerous teenagers to adult authors, as if those writers could serve as a new kind of nanny, ushering their progeny into the adult world. Adults would like to think that inasmuch as teenagers are reading, those books are helping them to get into college or to make adult decisions. A book or magazine directed at a teenager that engages adult issues is somehow more threatening than an adult text that ignores the teenager and treats the same themes. One is seduction; the other is a healthy stretch.

Here another kind of prejudice enters the scene. We are just entering the generation of parents who read real YA books as teenagers and now have teenagers of their own. Too many parents from earlier generations assume that any nonadult literature is just a weaker, watered down, less literary, thus less useful form of adult books. It would be the very rare parent who would say, "My sixteen-year-old wants to read adult books, but I really think he'd do better with Chris Lynch." The adult wants to hold him back to *Treasure Island* or send him on to *Cold Mountain*.

David Elkind, a professor of child and adolescent development, was quoted on the Internet describing another version of this strange squeeze, where parents want teenagers to grow up and yet also not be adult quite yet. "The spaces for adolescents have vanished. . . . Malt shops and soda fountains in drugstores are a thing of the past, as are large movie theaters. And though malls have proliferated, young people are not always welcome in these places. There are fewer and fewer places for young people just to congregate with friends. . . . At the same time, there has been an explosion of space for adults."

The one kind of space that there is for teenagers, and ever increasingly so, is in the media—on MTV, on WBN, on the radio, on the Web. Books could be, and magazines often are, that kind of space. They could offer a chance for congregating with friends, as teenagers discuss them, but few adults see them that way. Adults don't recognize the need for teenage physical space, and so they don't see the need for teenage cultural space.

Pat Hersch, the author of *A Tribe Apart* (Bantam, 1999), quotes one teenager as writing, "There is an unspeakable distance between youth and the grown-up world."

One reason for this distance can be found in Elkind's insight about the growth of adult territories. Adults keep expanding the psychological space they need for self-expression. Through confessional, memoir, therapy, and talk show, adults enter ever more deeply into their own conflicts over sexuality, abuse, relationships. They insist on working out their own adolescence as adults. All the more so as they go through divorces, with all of the antagonism they can bring, and create recombined families. But, at the very same time, these adults want their adolescent progeny to behave like children. They want rigid codes for schools, for literature, for behavior. What they are exploring in themselves is exactly what they want to prevent in their children.

That's one kind of parent. The other cannot set any standards at all, for they know all too well how they once broke their own parents' rules, and even now they struggle with their adolescent impulses. The sleazy saga of Monica and Bill, which reads like a bad YA novel, is a perfect example of this teenage adulthood writ large.

Whether through repression or resignation, adults simultaneously eclipse, erase, and ignore young people's reality. No wonder that, through college age, young people want institutions to set rules, to be in loco parentis for parents who weren't there before.

That harsh judgment leads directly to our third myth, "teenagers have no time for recreational reading." To fear, nostalgia, ignorance, and anxiety, we add rigidity. When I decided to hold this conference, I realized it was important to know what books schools assign to teenagers. I asked a librarian friend, Michelle Missner, to conduct surveys; I put out the question on the Web, and I learned about Arthur Applebee. He is a professor at SUNY-Albany who has studied in great detail the required reading in nearly every kind of high school in this country: urban and rural, large and small, private and public, secular and religious. Not only that, he's found similar studies dating back to the turn of the century. (For an entry point to Applebee's work, go to http://cela.albany.edu. From there you can navigate to read individual studies. Or see his 1993 NCTE Research Report, *Literature in the Secondary Schools: Studies of Curriculum and Instruction in the United States.*)

Applebee has found a core list of required books that is nearly invariant and nearly immobile. The most recent book on the list is *Lord of the Flies.* William Golding was the last one let on board, for his combination of insight and talent. He was, you might say, the final gift of the last large and powerful generation of liberal teachers. Just after that came the multicultural splits. Books were subject to communal judgment and taste. Any book that one group might like, another would protest, so teachers were happy to freeze required reading in the past and the deep past. An April 1998 article in *Language Arts* by Julie Wollman-Bonilla argued that middle school teachers and teachers in training most frequently objected to books that featured other than dominant beliefs or stressed racism or sexism as social problems. If you are going to eliminate such books, you have effectively blocked off modern literature.

Yet I'm not sure we should blame current teachers or overpraise prior generations. Applebee's long-term conclusion is that required reading in high school hardly ever changes; just a book or two is taken off every ten or twenty years, and another is added.

Individual schools and teachers are much more adventurous, but Applebee was looking at the core reading list, the heart of the heart of the high school experience. He has proven that schools have codified, made permanent, an absolute division separating what teenagers are assigned to read, what they experience in daily life, and the literature of their time.

I am not reviving that old fight between ancients and moderns. Personally, I am in favor of giving young readers a far greater exposure to classics. I just think they should read those classics alongside contemporary books. As several good teacher-oriented textbooks, such as *From Hinton to Hamlet* by Ted Hipple and Sarah Herz, make clear, old and new comment on each other. Instead we erect a wall between them. The one good thing about this wall is that it creates a hunger in teenagers for texts that do speak to them. If the classroom cannot provide that, they seek it in the library, on the Web, at the newsstand, or in the bookstore.

If we really believed that teenagers had so much to read for school that they couldn't read anything else, every one of us would be at our local school boards fighting to expand the required reading list. It is only because we know teenagers are not limited to what they are assigned that we can tolerate the sclerotic conditions of the schools.

The myths I've just described show how scared we are of teenagers, and how ignorant we are about what they are actually like, or could be if they had the chance to fulfill their potential. But there is something a bit dated about all of my finger waving. We are having this conference precisely because things are starting to change. Our sister media—television, music, magazines—have begun paying more attention to teenagers, and book publishers are all trying to figure out how to get into the act.

As many of you know, this year for the very first time the American Library Association will give out an award for the best book for readers ages twelve to eighteen, the Michael L. Printz Award, and the *LA Times* has already announced its first-time-ever prize for YA fiction. I even hear rumors that the chains might eventually reconsider their insane devotion to shelving teenage books deep inside the children's section. Could YA reviews in major newspapers be far behind?

What may, in the long run, prove even more exciting than any of our efforts is what is going on in the small but growing number of teenage reading groups. Whenever teenagers get to books, and get to talk about them, the results are amazing. I think that, with a little bit of organization, we could have a revolution on our hands, as groups of teenage readers around the country read books, discuss their reactions in person or by e-mail, and create a national conversation in which the prejudices of adults have almost no role. When teenagers read and talk, our most firmly held myths simply evaporate.

I began with myths precisely because we are now beginning to recognize these so-called truths as dubious, flawed, incomplete. The problem is we don't yet know what to replace them with, or how much truth they contain, or how to proceed once we wipe away our sleepy old habits. That is exactly what I hope we do today: isolate what is wrong, begin to think about what would be right, and leave in a fine state of puzzled excitement.

My charge to you is to listen to everything not just as a set of commentaries about teenagers, but as the beginning of a set of questions we need to ask ourselves. If we have not been able to pass on the culture of reading, why have we failed? If we haven't failed, why are we so worried? If we are so worried, why are we so resigned? I suspect that by the end of the day, even if we know nothing more about how to bring teenagers and reading together, we will know a great deal more about our own assumptions, beliefs, and attitudes. And, as we saw in the 1960s, consciousness-raising is always the best place to start.

[The main theme of the conference turned out to be how little was actually known about teenagers and reading. Academics reported the lack of good research on teenage reading, and the absence of any at all on how teenagers read on the Web. Librarians tracked the disconnect between teenagers' interests in, say, nonfiction, and the books that get starred reviews. Media analysts from MTV and Phillips (a leading manufacturer of interactive devices) disclosed surveys that showed reading to be much more popular among teenagers than anyone had expected. They also revealed that Gen-Y kids are eager for all sorts of ideas and experiences, if sometimes overwhelmed by them all. They are quite different from their bleak Gen-X older siblings, who were alienated from any form of media they did not create themselves. Teen magazine editors reported truly fabulous hit rates on their Web sites but had no clear policy on including book reviews in print or

online. Since then, one of the most popular magazines, TeenPeople, has given its name and support to a teenage book club.

The conference made clear that the long night of YA decline is ending. But that leaves it to us to clear away the encrustation of misinformation and mythology that had become enshrined as truth. That leads to a final question: why is it that publishing in general, and publishing for younger readers in particular, seems so prone to establishing "rules" that authors and editors, reviewers and librarians, treat as proven when their origins are murky, their validity is tested only by personal anecdotes, and they are rarely subject to public debate? If nothing else, I would urge readers of this book to question what they "know" to be "true" about teenage readers, and where that knowledge comes from.]

12

✛

Calling All Ye Printz and Printzesses

Now that we have an award for YA literature, we have to decide what we are rewarding. Figuring that out takes us back to the questions about the nature and purpose of YA that run through this whole book. In this talk to Michigan YA librarians, I used the language employed by the rules for the award to review those central themes: literature as art versus literature as developmental tool; adult projections and teenage realities; the glorious uncertainties that surround coming-of-age and its literature. But the strongest claim in this piece is that "popularity," so often favored as a measure of YA books, is not only intellectually indefensible but is really a stealth term disguising adult bias.

This year, more than seventy-five years after the Newbery was created and fifty years after the National Book Award was established, we finally have a prize devoted to books written for teenagers—the Michael L. Printz Award. Mike was, as some of you may know, a great YA librarian from Kansas who was serving his second term of duty on the ALA Best Books for Young Adults committee when he got seriously ill and then died. He stands for the best in librarianship—a true devotion to teenagers and books that made him both humble and impassioned. Mike was a kind of scoutmaster to the troop of YA book lovers, which is why we all miss him so much. The last time we spent together was at an ALA conference when he was already seriously ailing, but he was so eager to talk about books that he grabbed every second on a tedious fast food lunch line to do so.

I had a chance to serve on the Young Adult Library Services Association (YALSA) committee that lobbied for the Printz prize, and so I'd like to share with you what we hope it will be—the challenges and opportunities it presents. For everything about it relates directly to your jobs of working with teenagers.

The Printz will be announced during the midwinter ALA meeting each year, at the same press conference with all of the other major awards. We hope that the award comes to have the same weight as the other major library prizes—with the winner on TV and much discussion in the press and around the country. Yet we also wanted to make sure this prize was seen as different. While the Newbery, the Caldecott, and even the Batchelder are for readers up to the age of fourteen, the Printz is for readers aged twelve to eighteen, true teenage. And we want the award to reflect this difference. So we considered suggestions such as having our winner go on MTV instead of the *Today* show, holding the award banquet late at night at a club instead of in a safe hotel ballroom, or having it take place at a session with local teenagers. I don't think any of this will happen in the first year, but there is a publicity fund that should help get the word out. And I feel optimistic about press response. The Printz prize is not merely designed to honor a few books; it is meant to bring new attention to teenagers and reading. But in that effort it will merely be the final confirmation of a larger shift in perception that is already well under way.

I can't help feeling like a supporter of Columbus in 1492. Forever people have been telling us not to venture into publishing for teenagers, for the books are sure to fall off the edge of the world. No longer. Suddenly library directors, booksellers, publishers, critics, are starting to notice that middle-grade kids and younger teenagers have a tendency to age—to become older teenagers. The effect of this discovery is like adding the missing half of the globe—there is a scramble, almost a land rush, to reach these readers. Instead of being seen as terra incognita, teenagers are omnipresent, and nearly every effort to reach them has worked.

I have heard from local librarians in New York that Teen Read

Week was a big success. A major book club is about to launch a teen-age division and is sponsoring a nationwide contest to select fifteen teenagers a year to serve as paid book reviewers. The contest as much as the club is based on focus group studies that show a very active world of teenage reading. The Los Angeles *Times* now has a yearly award for best YA fiction. And there are two different YALSA projects that make use of teen reading groups—one designed to help them get books and galleys from publishers, the other an effort to create a shadow vote from teenagers on the previous year's BBYA list. This summer for the very first time we at Holt are going to send an author on a tour to teen reading groups. Even a sneaker company has added YA book reviews to its mail order catalog. Everywhere you look there is a changing perception of teenagers. Instead of being seen as difficult and unreachable, they are now treated as val-uable and nearly inescapable.

That sudden and rather ludicrous shift from must-avoid to pick-hit should serve as a warning, for there is no area in which there is more adult projection and misinformation than in dealing with teenagers. And that leads to my main topic today. For if we are cre-ating a book prize for teenagers, we have to decide what we are hon-oring. And to figure that out we have to enter the really scary area of our own adult assumptions.

I was also fortunate enough to serve on the YALSA committee that established the ground rules the Printz judges are to use. We agreed that the criteria had to be open-ended enough to encompass fiction, nonfiction, graphic novels as well as new styles not yet created, an-thologies, books with multiple authors, even books originally pub-lished overseas or in other languages. We wanted to be sure that the full range of publishing for teenagers, as well as the full spectrum of readers between the ages of twelve and eighteen, would be con-sidered. The only stipulation is that the books must have been pub-lished for younger readers. The Alex Award already honors adult books of interest to teenagers and we did not want to duplicate their efforts.

Because the categories are so wide open, we made a significant change from the rules for the Newbery. There, honors must be se-lected from among top vote-getters for the medal. As you may re-call, in 1998 there was only a single honor book, Richard Peck's *A Long Way from Chicago* (Dial, 1998). As I understand it, there were many other books that individual judges wanted to honor, but none were close enough in the final vote to be picked. Since the Printz is open to so many kinds of books, and since it is quite possible that a judge might feel that, say, an anthology or a biography is worthy of recognition but is not really a contender for the medal, we have split the vote. Once the medalist is determined, any book may be nominated for the up to four honor slots. In reverse, though, we also provided that if the judges do not feel there is a single extraordinary title that year, they may choose not to pick one at all.

While we changed the rules to reflect the diversity of YA readers and books, we did settle on one clear standard for the judges to use: this is an award for literary distinction. And that is where the rubber hits the road. For in trying to determine what literary distinction is for teenagers, we run right into the biggest split in the YA world, the tension between popularity, or teen appeal, and quality, which might also be called adult approval. I'm here to take sides in that argument.

In the YA world, nothing is as it appears to be. I've been attending meetings of the BBYA committee for more than a decade, and I've read about deliberations stretching back to the 1960s. In addition, I've seen more than my share of major reviews and library system evaluations and have heard or read many book reviews from teenagers. Running through this sea of commentary and evaluation is this endless debate between popularity and quality. This is so established a dichotomy that VOYA, and the whole VOYA review system that many teenage reading groups use, treats them as distinct and equally valid issues: "Q" and "P." But why? When we review books for younger children or for adults, indeed for any readers other than teenagers, we do not make this kind of hard distinction. What is it about books for teenagers that creates this duality in our judgment? And, even more important, what do we really mean when we use these terms?

Perhaps the most significant reason for this strange split is the nature of what teenagers are going through in adolescence. As a child, the individual is told he is special, she is loved. A child is treated both as an individual person and a part of a supportive family. Later, after high school, in college or at work, that person will be uprooted from home and family and will be judged entirely on his or her own merits. But in between is a strange time—almost like a calculus problem in which a set of discrete points "passes to the limit" and becomes a vector—in which the individual merges into the peer group. The individual seems to blur into the tastes, opinions, fashions, slang of the group.

Seeing this effect in action all around them in cliques of teenagers, librarians are especially eager for books that speak to the mores of the peer group. They want books to crack the code of teenage so that teenagers will accept them. There is something valid in that desire, and books that reach teenagers in that way do have a kind of literary distinction. The author has hit a difficult, fast-moving target. But it is a multileveled mistake to call that achievement "popularity."

Popularity is a measure of how many people like something. It treats the peer group model of teenage in its most generalized terms—as if teenage were a single group experience. Thus the literature that speaks most broadly to the most common teenage experiences is the best. This imposes on the endless varieties of adolescence a norm concocted in equal parts out of teenage sociology, the conventions of YA literature, and adult projections. Advocates of the importance of popularity see this measure as the voice of the people, a check against the imposition of adult values on teenage readers. But in practice, concern with popularity is the opposite of respect for teenagers. Instead, it judges art on the basis of stringent but unexpressed and untested adult assumptions. I have a very different sense of how to marry literary distinction and teenage experience. I see distinction in intimacy, which is almost the opposite of an aggregate number such as popularity.

One of the first things you notice if you listen to any group of teenage readers is how widely varied they are. Some congregate around the most popular or most articulate class member and copy her expressions or echo his tastes, while others share a love of Mercedes Lackey or Lurlene McDaniel, Robb Thomas or Neil Gaiman. Rather than a single universal voice there is a rich chorus of vocal lines. Listening to the BBYA discussions year after year, I'm struck by how this variation multiplies when you compare urban and rural high schools, rich and poor, coastal and heartland. Recently, in the wake of the Brooklyn Museum controversy, I gave a talk about avant-garde art to a New York city high school. Gazing out at the auditorium, I felt an overwhelming sense of coming home. These were the teenagers I grew up with, and they are very different from those I've met in suburban Arlington or New Orleans or San Francisco, or even just across the river in Englewood, New Jersey.

Still, there is at least one kind of reader that I've heard every time

I've listened to teenagers talk about books: exceptional readers who are clearly college bound. I've heard these readers praise novels because they unfolded slowly or had complex plots or featured thoughtful, intelligent characters. Immersed in the world of their reading with the same passion as the best graduate student or adult readers, they show levels of insight, knowledge, and comparative reading that are thrilling to hear. Nothing is beyond these readers. The fact that you can find these readers everywhere, in every high school, proves how wrongheaded it is to use popularity as a measure of literature.

If we associate excellence in YA books with describing average experiences in average ways and thus reaching average readers, we eliminate the readers who have the best chance of appreciating excellence. We need to trust that level of discernment rather than treat teenage abilities as the mean between the best and the worst. And this will lead to broader acceptance by other teenagers. As Peter Zollo explained teenage trends generally in his *Wise Up to Teens* (New Strategist, 1999), if the best readers believe in a book, they will become its advocates to the second best, and so on. A book for teenagers may be distinguished even if it takes a distinguished teenager to see that.

Certainly this is how awards work in the adult world. This year, for example, the Pulitzer Prize winner, Michael Cunningham's *The Hours* (Farrar, 1998), was a literary experiment framed by the suicide of Virginia Woolf, herself an experimental novelist. Winning the prize brought the book to a much wider audience.

I can imagine the howls of protest here, for there is a long-standing debate about awards in the library world: should they set high standards, even if that means many, even most, young readers will not enjoy the books? Or should they favor distinguished books with a broad readership? Every year this issue gets rehashed over the Newbery and the Caldecott. Since an award winner becomes a necessary purchase, some librarians favor books that are guaranteed not to sit on the shelf, while others are eager to reward books that over time may come to be recognized as trail-blazing contributions to the field.

It might be argued that an award for literary distinction should not be influenced by how the winning books are used but should only concern itself with the quality of the books. But some relativist is sure to question the basis of these standards. All the more so because there is a real egalitarian spirit in the YA world. Serving the underserved, identifying books for reluctant readers, avoiding judging readers' tastes in rigid and hierarchical ways are important to many YA librarians. They see up close how burdened students are with assigned texts that teachers and school boards claim are good for teenagers but have the appeal of literary cod liver oil.

I suspect that librarians, and the reviewers and award committees that serve them, want to see themselves as offering teenagers a bit of freedom, an island in which they and their opinions matter. Free reading helps teenagers develop their own taste, their own interests, their own selectivity. Imposing books on readers short-circuits this growth. Instead of discovering what they like, teenagers are forced to passively accept what they are given. Selecting a text that will be hard going for many readers as the very best book for young adults seems to violate this whole approach to reading and literature.

I think there is something else lurking behind the supporters of popularity that is not immediately evident in their words but still has a strong influence—I'm playing astronomer here, searching for evidence of a hidden planet by analyzing the weird orbit of a more familiar one. I believe the popularizers are reacting against a whole other crew: those who believe the mission of all books for young readers, especially those for endangered and dangerous teenagers, is moral instruction. The Moral Instruction gang believe the test of the value of a YA book is the values it supposedly teaches or the role models it theoretically offers or the "realistic hope" it gives to angst-ridden readers.

If that is the lead weight on literature that the popularizers are trying to jettison, then we're in the struggle together. In stressing literary distinction, the award committee was explicitly and firmly rejecting that entire agenda. If we want teenagers to learn civics, to gain self-esteem, to develop critical thinking, to be more open to others, these are lessons we as adults need to teach them directly at home, in class, or in after-school activities. Books work one to one, text to reader, and in strange unpredictable ways. All we can do is seek books that are distinguished and be there to help teenagers who read them to make sense of the thoughts and feelings they inspire. If we wanted to give an award for best printed sermon, we would have done so.

Do you see the strange space we are getting into? We created an award for literary distinction—which is a most abstract standard—

but the fact that the award will come from a library division enmeshes it in the conflicts over the nature of reading, books, and the special place of books in the lives of young people that are endemic to the library community.

That brings me back to the popularity problem. One way in which many reviewers and librarians try to heal the breach between their commitment to abstract ideas of excellence and their desire to honor teenagers' free choices is by adding another term to the mix—potential popularity. This concept seems to join the two sides, and there is something to that, but in the end I think it is a trap that exposes the flaw in this entire system of evaluating YA literature.

Quality certainly can yield popularity. Quality, you might say, is the author's ability to go deeper, higher, or further—more insightful, more lyrical, more challenging, more revealing, funnier, more unsparing, more thought-provoking—than most. That means the book is capable of opening up a reader, showing her things in herself she didn't know were there. The book is not popular because it gives the reader what he knows he wants but because it changes, it transforms, who he knows himself to be. This doesn't mean that excellence is limited to highly interior literary fiction. Any book that does something exceptionally well expands a reader's horizons. Potential popularity, then, is another way of saying "good book." Or good book aided by good book talk.

The problem is, who determines which books have this potential, and how does he or she make that judgment? Since the evaluation of worth—quality—is still hedged in terms of acceptance—popularity—the reviewer has free reign to act on all of her own tastes and biases without having to defend them directly. This is the heart of my problem with the whole idea of judging anything by "popularity." It is most often a way to smuggle in prejudice, limited experience that has become enshrined as wisdom, and adult bias under the false banner of concern with teenagers.

One of the most frequent comments I hear and read is that "teenagers won't get" this or that situation or character. This is used as a judgment of books that use unfamiliar slang, complicated plots, borrowings from science, or really anything that the adult reading the book stumbles over. I think "teenagers won't get it" most often means, "I didn't get it, and so I believe this creature, this teenager, who I am inventing as a smaller and stupider version of myself, surely won't." A seeming judgment of probable popularity is actually a projection of adult limitation.

In listening to teenagers, I have often found them to be much more open and curious than adults expect. They are living in a world we created and we impose on them. Most of what they experience is at least half insane. They constantly have to translate from our language, our assumptions, our expectations, our standards into theirs. An odd book in which the language, the situations, the assumptions require some work is just another new thing to get used to. As one teenager at a BBYA session said about a long fantasy adults feared would be hard to get through, "No, I liked it because it was a good story." Being a good story, not those adult checklists of teenage likes and dislikes, is what mattered to him. Fearful adults wanting acceptance from the generalized teenage peer group guess at its likes and dislikes. They then turn those surmises into lists of YA commandments, which only further distance them from the rich variety of YA experiences.

If we all sat here and thought for a few minutes, I bet we could come up with a great list of so-called truths about teenage readers that are spoken in the YA world with the certitude of a pre-Copernican astronomer asserting that the earth is the center of the universe. Many may have bits of truth to them or may have begun as individual perceptions, but, even though they contradict themselves, they have become enshrined as universal truths. And no dispassionate researcher has actually gone out to measure how true they are. For example, boys don't read; boys won't read girl books; teenagers won't read about kids who are younger than they are; teenagers hate the term YA; teenagers hate the term teenager; teenagers can't follow flashbacks; teenagers don't like poetry; teenagers like poetry; teenagers don't like unfamiliar slang; teens prefer realism; teens prefer fantasy; teens prefer humor; teenagers prefer adult books; teenagers only like paperbacks; teenagers only like short books.

I'm sure some teenagers fit every one of these descriptions. It may even be that most teenagers fit most of them. But that tells us absolutely nothing about how a given book will be received. That depends on the book, and all of this shorthand is merely a substitute for actually weighing out how it does or doesn't work. The less we question these beliefs, the more dangerous they can be.

One of the most telling examples of this mismatch between adult assumption or projection and teenage experience came up at the last ALA midwinter meeting, when a large group of teenagers were discussing two books, David Blatner's *The Joy of Pi* (Walker, 1997), and

Hans Magnus Enzensberger's *The Number Devil* (Metropolitan, 1998). Many adults shivered at the mere mention of the books. Math was a subject they hated, were glad to see the last of, and from which they believed they had a safe distance in going to library school. Assuming teenagers were similar types, they could hardly read, much less consider the books. The teenagers, a very mixed set of boys and girls, younger and older, from many ethnic backgrounds, were much more open to the books. They all take math, and it is part of their given reality. A book that makes math interesting was a real boon, filled with exciting surprises. To the adults, math was a topic to be avoided and therefore probably not popular with teenagers. To the teenagers, it was a fact of life that can be handled in better or worse ways.

The dirty little secret of a great deal of YA reviewing is that the reader the adult has in mind is a female teenage bookworm quite similar to the person that reviewer once was. That is fine as a subset of teenage, but when it is invisibly projected out as teenage in general, it obscures rather than reveals teenage experience.

The best place to see that is in the whole area of books for boys. Because of shifts in our larger culture, topics that were for thousands of years thought crucial for young males, and for over a hundred made up a great deal of reading for adolescent males, have come under deep suspicion. I'm thinking, for instance, of books about war in which there is a sense of heroism and nobility, of courage and self-sacrifice, of bloodlust, passion, and patriotism. That tone is confined to graphic novels, where we somehow find it acceptable, or to books about women or members of minority groups who distinguished themselves in serving their country. I am not eager to return to the days of John Wayne movies or Robert Hogan's *G-8 and His Battle Aces,* but this is a clear case where possible popularity is totally trumped by invisible but powerful adult attitudes. For example, if the D-Day scene in *Saving Private Ryan* were in a YA book, I'm sure it would have avid readers. Yet many adults would be uncomfortable about promoting it to teenagers.

An even more egregious victim of adult assumptions is nonfiction. As Dr. Betty Carter learned in two studies, one of library circulation statistics and another of starred reviews, nonfiction is the most popular area of teenage reading, and yet such books are least likely to be considered necessary purchases by librarians. This is so true that we have hardly begun to develop standards for what distinction in YA nonfiction would mean. There are obvious check-lists—does the book have back and front matter, notes, sources, clear illustrations with good captions—and a general desire for the narrative to read well. But these are minimum conditions, not marks of distinction. Truly distinguished nonfiction admits its limitations and invites readers into a process of discovery. Like the best literary fiction, it is willing to be ambiguous and to leave space for the reader's own conclusions.

Carter noticed something else in her most recent research that clashes with another set of adult assumptions, and brings us right up to the present. Five years ago she wrote a history of trends in twenty five years of selections by the BBYA committee, *Best Books for Young Adults: The History, the Selection, the Romance* (ALA, 1994). I spoke at the preconference where her work was presented and one of the distinguished editors there made a categorical assertion: YA ends at fourteen. After that, we lose readers to adult books. This year Carter has just completed looking at what has changed in the past five years. Her main conclusion is that while the committee is selecting fewer and fewer adult books, YA books are aiming older and older, and now the full spectrum of teenage is represented. So be careful of your assumptions about teenagers and reading. You never know when fast-changing realities are going to undermine your long-held but unexamined beliefs.

The new books that Carter has been looking at often rest on the outer edge of YA literature. These books challenge readers to think for themselves. And I believe this is where teenagers can truly enter into books. Here, where their reactions are personal and individual, not generalized into stereotypes or enshrined as YA dos and don'ts, is where each reader's experience counts. To return to my main theme, the issue of literary distinction, the term we should be looking for is not popularity but intimacy. Does a book have the potential to touch readers deeply so that, in the struggle with it, they begin to see and to shape themselves?

I suspect that literary distinction for teenagers, whether in fiction or nonfiction, will most often arise in texts that have a great deal to offer but also allow space for the reader to enter. These are books that challenge, engage, provoke, tease, disturb, beguile, entice, seduce. They inspire readers but do not provide handy resolutions. They let the reader enter the text—in an engagement that is different from the generalized sum total we call popularity. The individual adds in her own experience, his own insight, to complete the story.

This approach to teenage readers is very evident in some recent books that I'd like to mention to you. Walter Dean Myers's *Monster* (Harper, 1999) and Paul Fleischman's *Mind's Eye* (Holt, 1999) are a very interesting pair. Myers's novel is in the form of both a film script and a narrative, and Fleischman's is a play. While both have clear stories, both leave a great deal to the judgment of the reader. Is Steve really a monster, as the prosecution claims? That is the central question in Myers's book, and it is one each reader must decide individually. There is enough evidence to know what part he probably played in a botched robbery that turned into a shooting. But that does not really solve the larger question of what a monster, a criminal, a danger to society is. The only way for the reader to know is to follow Steve's own belief that movies reveal a kind of truth. So what truth has his movie shown?

Fleischman's book centers on an imaginary trip that an eighty-eight-year-old woman in a nursing home convinces a sixteen-year-old paraplegic to take with her. Guided by a 1910 Baedecker, they journey to Italy, where the teenager's inner life begins to be expressed in her perception of herself as a monster, a Medusa—though it also provides an opportunity for her to imagine what love could be. The ending of the book, in which the teenager continues the trip without the older woman, can be seen in two possible ways—as leaving her trapped in fantasy or as the first step in true mental healing.

There is something very contemporary and very true in the way both books recognize the depth of darkness within teenagers and yet also assume that readers have the intelligence and the imagination to deal with ambiguity. Neither author felt it necessary to spell out a moral, a message—actually both hinted at messages that they also undermined. Neither author had to supply a clearly happy ending—though you could argue that both end happily. Neither feared losing readers by moving away from a single narrative. Actually, in both cases the experimental form of the piece is at the heart of the book. Both authors trusted that young readers are experienced enough with dialogue, with theater, with TV, with film to make sense of a novel cast in those forms.

I am not suggesting that we equate literary quality with books that have ambiguity or multiple narrators. But I do see the willingness of two of the most established authors to take these risks as a sign of a maturing field that has many kinds of distinction in it. We don't need people to copy these masters. Rather, we need to see their example as a sign of what is possible and that risks are worth taking.

Switching over to nonfiction, I am going to hazard being in really bad taste by talking about what I've tried to do with the biography of Sir Walter Ralegh that is coming out this year. Again I'm not saying this is the standard, or even that I've achieved what I set out to do—that is up to all of you to decide. But what I wrestled with as an author is relevant to anyone tackling nonfiction for teenagers today.

The central issue in the book is how Ralegh and more generally the English saw the New World. The answer fits neither the old heroic mold of the stories we used to read nor the debunking tone of the angry critiques that have come out since the 1960s. All too human, Ralegh yearned to conquer what he saw as virgin lands ripe for the plucking and yet felt a kind of reverence for their unspoiled beauty. I think showing him to be a complex individual is much more important for my readers than trying to shoehorn him into the role of hero or villain. We no longer need biographies that offer uplift and moral instruction about role models. They can be deeply human engagements with real three-dimensional people. Perhaps that is now all they can be.

In an age when every teenager knows about the president's sex life, can figure the exact dollar worth of every sports hero, and is up to the minute on the tears and traumas of every music star, it would be incongruous to suggest that people in the past were flawless. Moreover, teenagers growing up in families that have split apart and recombined already know a great deal about how an adult can be good yet flawed, and how every story has more than one side.

Growing up, I always assumed the past took place in black and white and was populated solely by older people. I hope that the biography of an important yet imperfect person can connect young readers to the past, rather than split it off from them.

And, in turn, I expect readers to see my story in many different ways, which is why the notes tell them where I learned everything I know, so that they can set off on their own journeys of discovery.

Judging books by the average reader blocks that individuality, substituting a generalized image of the teenager for real teenagers with all of their mischief and intelligence. We adults can only reach individuals if we, as individuals, stand up for what we believe in and invite reactions to that. Rather than disguise our biases and beliefs by putting them in the mouths of young readers, we should stand up for what we think the literature of adolescence should be. Then let teenagers react to that. Let them challenge our assumptions.

I hope that this teenage engagement carries through the whole process of the Printz Award. Once a winner and the honor books are selected, let the debates begin. Let adults defend their choices and listen to teenagers' responses. Let a choice, be it an easy read or a tough stretch, be the beginning of a national dialogue. Let each side hone its sense of distinction in open-ended discourse with the other. Distinction is neither an unquestionable decree from on high nor a false bow to vox pop. Instead, it emerges out of an ongoing dialogue in which adults, based on their knowledge and experience, propose standards and defend exemplars, which teenagers shape and are shaped by as they react to them.

YA literary distinction is likely to prove to be as varied as teen readers themselves, and as open-ended as their question-filled lives. Evaluating books by this standard is much more difficult than estimating popularity, and far more rewarding.

13

✣

Puff the Magic Dragon: How the Newest Young Adult Fiction Grapples with a World in Upheaval

> Though they were not planned as joint pieces, this essay is, in a sense, the application of some of the ideas I discussed in the last chapter to five recent YA novels. Fortunately, we no longer have to argue that the YA novel deserves to exist. Now we can talk about the books themselves. This essay was published as the lead piece in a special issue of the *Los Angles Times Book Review* that was devoted to education and books for young people.

Between the spate of school shootings that culminated in Littleton, the panic over how to raise girls (and then boys), and the success of adolescent-oriented movies and TV shows, teenagers have erupted into the national consciousness. Whether as a crisis or as a golden revenue stream, they are suddenly all over the media. Moreover, just as we adults adjust to the digitalizing of our world, we sense that young people are almost a different species, bred to flourish in a multimedia environment. Looking out at these strange creatures, teenagers, adults seem unsure whether to be scared of them or for them; whether to try harder to protect them from the world we have created or trust that they will make better use of it than we have. Have we given them too much freedom and cyber access, or not enough of our all-too-busy selves?

One of the best ways to see into the fragile yet vibrant world of teenagers is through coming-of-age fiction, for often authors sense and can give form to interior lives that are invisible to the rest of us. But until recently, few looked to young adult novels to encompass rapidly changing realities. All too often they were addicted to an insistently narcissistic first-person present tense voice, trapped within the conventions of a two-dimensional brand of "realism." No longer. The best new YA novels are finding how to bring the explosion of media narratives within the borders of bound books, giving young readers a space to recognize their imperiled and empowered selves. For teenagers self, text, and voice have all gone multimedia wild. Here, in ever increasing increments of weirdness, are some recent novels that explore that world.

Bruce Brooks's new novel *Vanishing* (Laura Geringer Books/ Harper Collins, 1999) is about two characters in a hospital—Alice, a girl who is wasting away from a hunger strike and bronchitis, and Rex, a boy with an unnamed terminal disease. From the first we see how she is experiencing her state: "I hardly sleep at all. I—I just kind of shimmer beneath the sheets, see, and sort of glow through the night." To which Rex responds, "You're entirely too poetic—and too *bad* at it—to be *really* sick."

Brooks offers elegant, lyrical phrases, undermined by a tough-talking practicality. You have to pay attention to words, how they hypnotize and what they actually mean, to see where he is going. Writing a book that is so attentive to language shows a level of trust in his young readers that is typical of Brooks but is relatively uncommon among YA writers. Though Brooks's young characters are seriously ill, they, and the readers they stand for, are not the most damaged figures in the book.

In one sense, Alice is vanishing, aiming to turn herself into light. But in another it is the adults who have vanished from her; she emulates them in attempting to both transcend and obliterate herself. Her mother is an alcoholic, her father a weak man who kicked Alice out of the house to quiet his domineering mother. In Brooks's universe adults cannot see young people and have little to offer them but the acting out of their own weaknesses. In their harsh dramas of life and death, it is the young people who are the Hunger Artists in adults' Kafkaesque world. Nevertheless, Brooks's straightforward narrative is well within the boundaries of conventional fiction.

Moving a step away from those secure shores, we come to what I'd deem the classicists of the new YA fiction: Robert Cormier and Paul Fleischman. Cormier's latest book, *Frenchtown Summer* (Delacorte, 1999), might at first seem an odd entry in this lineup of experimental fiction. It is about a sensitive boy during a Depression-era summer in a French-Canadian New England factory town. Told in a series of first-person prose poems, each of which adds up to a chapter, it is a kind of adolescent *Our Town* in which Eugene's dawning sexuality brings with it an increasing sensitivity to the secrets of the adults around him.

As in *Vanishing*, it is the father who is shadowy: "My father was a silhouette/as if obscured/by a light shining behind him." While Eugene, a Catholic, has a sense of sin for the secrets that do not make it to the confessional, the larger evils are outside of him. What is saving to him, and to the book as a whole, is a poetic sensibility. What could be a novella or a short story has been stripped down to evocative lines that could easily be read as a radio play. As in Karen Hesse's *Out of the Dust* (Scholastic, 1997), Cormier has risked reducing a tale to its essence, to poetry, and so has made a quite traditional story entirely fresh. Stripping a story to bare poetic lines lets in room for illustrations, and each chapter features Rockwell Kent–like images that add to the sense of clean-edged, if harsh, Americana.

Paul Fleischman takes this process of distilling prose one step further in *Mind's Eye* (Henry Holt, 1999). Like *Vanishing*, the book is set in a ward where, in the main, only two characters carry the story. But here there is no narration at all. On one level, the novel proceeds entirely in dialogue and is meant to be performable as a play. Fleischman has pushed the novel even further toward pure voice and away from the calm assurance of a narrator's guiding hand. On another, though, the book does not take place on the page at all.

In the progress of the novel, Elva, an eighty-eight-year-old woman who is losing her sight, begs a new resident at a convalescent home, Courtney, a sixteen-year-old girl with a severed spinal cord, to read to her from a 1910 Baedeker guide. Elva wants them to take an imaginary journey to Italy together—along with her long dead husband. As Elva and Courtney take their trip, readers fill in the details in their own minds, guided perhaps by the bits of Baedeker maps reproduced in the book.

Even as he turns readers over to their imaginations, Fleischman makes his most dramatic break from conventional YA fiction. Measured against the world of electronic distractions and games of erotic entanglement she has grown up with, Courtney believes she has become a monster, a Medusa, "because I'm as ugly as she is." Invention is as dangerous as it is liberating. In this YA world, the threats are no longer out there, they are in here: "I have it inside me. I have the Evil Eye."

Which brings us to two baroque books. Walter Dean Myers's latest is *Monster* (HarperCollins, 1999). As with Fleischman, this book abandons a reassuring external narrator and gives us instead a kind of script. But where *Mind's Eye* looks back from the novel to poetry and theater, *Monster* moves ahead to film and television. The whole novel is a mental film Steve Harmon is writing as he waits out a trial for murder.

According to the prosecution, Stephen was meant to case out a Harlem corner store, give the all-clear, and then get part of the profits when a couple of older, tougher kids pulled off an easy theft. The robbery was bungled, and in the fracas the store owner was killed with his own pistol. A couple of jailhouse tips led the police to the two main suspects, and then on to Steve.

Steve is a smart sixteen-year-old who goes to an elite New York public high school, and he particularly loves film. He sees a kind of truth in what a filmmaker records. So his mental film is a test: is he the monster the prosecution describes him as being, the monster he sees in jail in the faces and fights all around him, or is he the loved and loveable child his parents knew him to be?

As in *Mind's Eye*, the evil is in Steve, or, if it is not, good and evil are just the many narratives, the many spins, that adults, the media, the courts impose on young people—and, in this case, especially, a young black male. There is no self, really, outside of all of the spinning, just the film record of the debate. There are enough clues to suggest what Steve actually did do on the day of the robbery but not enough to determine whether those actions add up to making him a monster. Both the adolescent reader and the adolescent protagonist must decide for themselves how to piece together life's competing and overwhelming narratives.

There is a strange crisscross in these books: as the space for the individual, the emerging adolescent, the narrator's voice diminishes to the vanishing point, the books open up. The spot art in *Frenchtown Summer*, the map fragments in *Mind's Eye*, become in *Monster* a book in which design is part of the story, and many kinds of art fill the pages. The author's son, Christopher, a talented artist in his own right, made the images and is listed as one of the creators of the book. If young people are losing a sense of self to the onslaught of the media, they are also being freed to find themselves in words and images, in novels that are performances or scripts.

This moment of simultaneous crushing and freedom leads us to *Making Up Megaboy* (DK Publishing, 1998), by Virginia Walter and illustrated by Katrina Roeckelein. As in *Monster*, Robbie Jones is in jail. Here there is no doubt: he killed a Korean liquor store owner, using his father's gun to do it. But why? The entire book is a set of statements from the people in his life, matched with art that is evocative of them or is by him.

He and his only friend, Ruben, had drawn a comic strip, *Megaboy*, and some of their art flits through the pages as well. The psychological dynamics in this book are the least sophisticated of the books we have examined: Robbie is clearly lonely and has a crush on a classmate, and she is quite the self-preoccupied airhead. Yet *Megaboy* is the extreme case of this new field of YA fiction in which the media frees but obliterates young people. Here all narratives are equal; a child's own working out of who he is holds no special place against everything everyone tells him he is. A secure world of concerned adults has vanished entirely, to be replaced by professionals with agendas: reporters and cops, lawyers and doctors. The strange effect of *Megaboy*, like all of these books, is a kind of exhilaration, an almost at-the-circus excitement, at the ways in which books are opening up to allow in visuals, other media, and other narratives, mixed with a dire sense of fear for where the self can be found amid all the sound and fury.

In the new YA novel, and the new YA reality, adults vanish and intrude, media crushes and frees. This makes for an exciting time in fiction. It will be up to young people, as they read and react to these books, to tell us what it is like to live.

14

✚

What Is YA, and What Is Its Future: Voice, Form, and Access—A Dialogue with Jacqueline Woodson

To my regret, Jackie and I have done only one book together, an anthology of African American writings about coming-of-age called *A Way Out of No Way* (Holt, 1996). But one of the perks of my profession is the many chances I have to meet authors like Jackie at conferences, parties, and the homes of mutual friends. There, freed from the pressure of this book or that deadline, we get to debate, puzzle out, and gossip about the world we both inhabit. Aside from being one of the most important authors who writes about teenagers, Jackie is one of the most subtle critics of the field. If this dialogue offers no final answers, I hope it at least allows others to eavesdrop on her mind at work, and on the tennis match of editors and authors at play.

Jackie is a writer first, and she brings that depth of literary craft, engagement, and training to the whole problem of writing for teenagers. But she is also an engaged political thinker who can see YA literature in the larger context of the cultural conflicts of our time. Aside from that, talking with her is fun. Here, together, we try to define the borders of our field. But in the process, we also come to grips with what YA literature is.

Marc Aronson: I think the main thing about teenagers is that adults totally ignore them or are in a total panic about them. Teenagers don't exist—or let's have a national conference on the problem of teenagers and, whatever, pregnancy, AIDS, violence. Adults have a sense of Teenage, but always tied to a feeling of Crisis.

What is the limit of YA? Is there any limit? Is it a thematic limit? A stylistic limit? What is the edge?

Jacqueline Woodson: Are you asking what is the edge for young adults or for adults? I think there definitely is an edge. I am thinking of a book that I might write called *Fucking White Boys*. If there were a book with this title, would it ever get published? Would it ever get into the world? Would teenagers read it? Of course they would, in a minute, but would they have access to it? No.

I always think of teenagers as being about five steps—which means they are probably ten steps—ahead of us. And yet we are scrambling to abort the "teenage crisis" or get control over it, our own adult control over it. Teenagers themselves are limitless. I think they would read anything.

They would read a book entirely written in red on beige paper, something that we would not look at twice because it would hurt our eyes and it would make us do too much work. But they are so much more open than we are.

MA: Most of what is said about books for teens is a set of negative rules. You can't do this because kids won't like it. Or you can't have too much slang. Or you can't be too long. Or you can't have more than one narrator. Or you can only have more than one narrator. These are all a set of restrictions. Yet you are talking about how teenagers are more open than we are. We are trying to meet that openness by guessing the restrictions.

Do you think the reason you couldn't publish the novel you just described is the title or the content?

JW: I think both. I'd hit a wall around the title. Then I'd hit a wall around the content. I'm sure I could get some small press or some teenage zine to publish it in parts. It would get out to young people that way. But with my mainstream mind, I couldn't publish it. I doubt if a review would show up in *Horn Book*, or if it would be on an ALA best books list. For a writer that is something I really need to think about and come to terms with, because I don't want that to be my limit.

MA: You are saying that if you had an IV going straight from your brain to teenagers' souls, it would carry no limit.

JW: Right.

MA: But you are also saying there are limits to what the existing structures will allow. And that matters to you because you want your books to have a mainstream presentation—you don't want your work to be lost on the edges or posted on the Web for someone to find.

But then, if the structures of the YA world hold an author back, *should* there be young adult publishing? Why not publish this theoretical book as an adult book and leave it to teenagers to find?

JW: One way to answer that is to look at a quintessential YA book like *Ruby* by Rosa Guy [Bantam, 1992]: it is edgy because it is about lesbianism; it is about being young adult, and it stays in a young adult framework. It has short chapters, short sentences, it is a narrow book. Compare that to Sandra Cisneros's *House on Mango Street* [Arte Publico, 1983], which crossed over from adult, and yet a young person can pick it up and see a young voice, a young self in it. There is a need for both kinds of books.

MA: You are speaking about voice and form.

JW: And access.

MA: Yes. So much of what teenagers are getting that is not from friends or off the Web is coming through adults. A young adult section in a bookstore is really important to parents who are choosing books for their kids. Teenagers still live in a world defined by adults, so you need to have something that reassures parents and teachers. The symbol "YA" is a kind of camouflage to get things past the intervening adult world.

JW: A lot can happen in YA lit that can be really subversive. Adults read the flap copy and say okay. But the real stuff gets there. It gets to the young people.

MA: So YA is voice, form, access. Where can each of these categories go next? Where can each of them be pushed? For example, it used to be said that the YA novel had to be in the first person. Now we are in a phase where novels are done in dual voices or multiple voices. Do you see a new kind of voice?

JW: I see going much further beyond that, with everybody having their say.

MA: A kind of Rashomon situation.

JW: I think something like that might be confusing to adults, while young people's minds are open. Teenagers can completely handle the Internet, with access coming in from everywhere and from all types of media. So multiplicity is one place things could go, in terms of voice.

I think happy endings have been out the window for a long time, and that was a theory that was out there: a book had to have some kind of complete whole happy ending. It does have to have a wholeness to it, but it doesn't have to be happy.

MA: I have a great story to tell about that. I was at a conference in which teenagers and adults divided up into groups to discuss books, and our group was talking about John Marsden's *Letters from the Inside* [Houghton Mifflin, 1994]. The adult who was leading the conversation felt that the book was disturbing, was less than successful, because it did not have a happy ending. One brilliant teenager objected: "Why does the happiness have to come in the ending?" She pointed out that there were great emotional exchanges in the book, and she didn't see why they have to come at the sunset, when the characters walk happily off to their future.

JW: Excellent.

MA: That's voice and ending, what about form? *Fucking White Boys*—was that a mandate, a manual, or a curse? Which valence did you want it to have?

JW: That's what the beauty of it is; it could be any one of those. You won't know until you read the book.

MA: So here is a boundary of content—which would violate access. Kids would never get to it.

JW: From the title on.

I wonder, are we moving to a place where a word like "fucking" is not going to be the curse that it is today? I hear "ass" all over the place, even on TV sitcoms. It blows me away. Four years ago I would never have heard that word out there like that.

MA: We just published *The Adventures of Blue Avenger* [Henry Holt, 1999]. It is a sweet book, not a graphic novel, though the main character both draws one and becomes a kind of superhero. When he curses, the author puts in symbols like exclamation points, as they did in old comics. But one teacher has an exercise where students have to bring in a word and she parses it. One day she calls on Blue's friend, who is totally unprepared, and mutters, "Oh shit." The teacher then says, "OK, let's analyze that," and she does.

So here is this very sweet, funny, decent book, with a whole scene centering on this one word. I asked the reviewers how are you going to review it? In a starred *SLJ* review, the reviewer wrote "analyzes 'shit.'"

JW: Really, they wrote the "s" word?

MA: They did. I thought that was fair. You can't criticize the author for having it in the book if you won't put it in your journal. If the reviewers would be willing to quote the title of your book, then they could have at it.

JW: That is the point, getting to the place where they would even put my title into print.

MA: Moving on to voice, you've taken on the issue of whether "you have to be it to write it." How can you know points of view that are not your own? Is there another borderline there, a next place?

JW: When I think of other voices I think for me, as a black person, it is about appropriation. Like the young people who take on the dress modes and dancing and music of blacks, but are still prejudiced. You dig your own grave as a writer when you take chances like that where you might not have all of the information.

But I wonder whether because our culture is changing it is more about appropriation, rather than really getting to know a people. Right now South Asian is the big appropriation. The music and the religion and the fusion of the music with our music. People say, "Oh, they are so spiritual," but what do they really know about this culture?

MA: I think we are in the age of mixedness: racially, like people who investigate their own family trees and find out that they have a black side of the family that they never acknowledged, or mixedness within oneself, and within our culture.

I think the years from the sixties to the eighties were about identity, about roots and coming out: "I embrace who I truly was all along and didn't admit." I think the narrative now is about ambiguity. It is not about being a stable self; it is about being a complex self.

Identity is about community. You embrace this self-definition and then you are part of the community. Can you build community that is not so well-defined? Can it be more ambiguous, more unstable?

JW: I think you are right, and that is where my generation gap is going to come.

MA: Come on Jackie, you can't have a generation gap!

JW: I know it is going to happen.

MA: You will run into people who are like mercury, totally unstable and comfortable being everything.

JW: And I will throttle them—and say "You have to decide!" You know my brother's biracial, and I grew up with this idea that was passed down from slavery: one drop of black blood made you black. My brother was black, even though he looks more Mediterranean. But then anyone who had a little bit of black blood was considered black. Now that is not the case. Chris Myers and I were talking about this, because he's biracial, but he identifies as black.

Now, so many biracial people I know are saying, "I am going to claim both things." And I say, "But you are black."

MA: Also since the immigration laws changed in 1965, new people so flooded the old categories. We were comfortable with those boundaries—black or white, and we kind of squinted on Asian or Indian. That was not a large enough issue to really worry about. But after 1965 you have all of these Hispanics coming who don't fit, dark-skinned people from South Asia who don't fit. That puts pressure on our categories and makes us rethink everything that neatly fit into black or white. Now it's clear everybody else around here doesn't fit into salt or pepper. People would rather be human, not salt or pepper.

One of the critics said to me that we haven't had a really good novel on bisexuality. It's the same sense of ambiguity.

JW: It is so true, and the same argument. It used to be the Gay and Lesbian Parade, then Gay Lesbian, and Bisexual, then Gay, Lesbian,

Bisexual, and Transgender. But the whole argument in the gay and lesbian community—which also fits with the race issue—is the point of access. It wasn't the part of you that is into heterosexual relationships that is getting oppressed, it was the part that was queer. And when you marched in the queer parade, that was the part you were embracing. And they respond, "No, we want people to know we are both things." But why? What kind of access are you getting?

MA: But I think you are speaking exactly for that generation gap.

JW: Yup.

MA: Because one argument is against a monovision world, saying, "Yes there is an 'other' to your picture." Now there is an "other" to the "other."

Back to our theme. We talked about access and voice; now what about style? What aspects of style are not permitted in YA or will become permitted, or should be? You were saying the other night that the unreliable narrator is a problem. What do you see in adult writing that you think you can't do in YA, or is there anything?

JW: What I would like to do is to use a lot fewer words.

MA: Fewer?

JW: I would like to be much more implicit.

MA: Why? I think one of your great strengths is being so . . .

JW: Being such a minimalist? We still give young people too much. We don't think they will come to the novel, so we bring it to them. I'm not sure if I would use informal language. I don't even know if I'd have more sex in my books, if I could. There is a part of my brain that is shut off because for so long I've been a good girl. I've played by the rules. I don't know what is in me if I didn't.

MA: Jackie, you are putting yourself almost at opposite ends of the spectrum—toying with a title like *Fucking White Boys*, which is as aggressive as you can be, and pondering what would you do with sexuality if you really let out all of the stops. Yet on the other hand you are talking about being all the more implicit, all the more silent, more terse. You say, and I agree, YA tends to give too much. There is this pressure to go all the way, 100 percent, toward the reader.

JW: If you are much more implicit, readers have to bring their own experience to it. I am giving you my version. If I am talking about something like sex, what I am bringing is my own experience. But if I say less, readers don't have to read mine and come to their judgments based on mine; they can assume that I am thinking about such and such based on what they have experienced.

MA: Very smart. This gets back to the very beginning, about being steps behind the teenagers: the effort to be a teenager, exactly where they are, is probably going to be wrong. But the effort to give them someplace to enter, with themselves, is right.

JW: Definitely.

MA: Give them an entry point that they can fill.

You imagine an author pushing on both ends, toward the expressed and toward the restrained. What about format? Do you have impulses to write graphic novels or to do zines, other new things?

JW: Because I don't draw, even though I see things in my head a lot, it would be hard. There is this urgency to graphic novels that I can do in adult, but I can't make that cross over to YA. There is this visual side that is difficult for me, like going from a novel to a screenplay.

MA: What about film?

JW: Well, I am doing film now. I can visualize that because a lot of it is dialogue driven. When you have a good film, it is all about subtext.

MA: Subtext is an issue of access because reviewers are inconsistent on it. Some are very alert and attuned to it; some are totally mystified and therefore rule that kids will not get it. This is a place where you have adult obstruction.

JW: Exactly. I like that, "adult obstruction."

MA: I think we are afflicted by it. You deal a lot with teachers. Do you see kids' writings too?

JW: I see their letters. I just got the most telling letter, from a girl who had read *From the Notebooks of Melanin Sun* [Scholastic, 1995]. "Dear Jackie Woodson, I got a bunch of books for Christmas and

Melanin Sun was one of them, and the first thing I thought was I am not going to read any of these books." And so my first thought was *Melanin Sun* is not a book you just give somebody, so there is something going on. Then she said, "I don't know a lot about gay people, I don't think about them that much, I swear I don't. If my mother was gay I don't know what I'd do, I'd probably do just what Melanin Sun did, I'd punch walls, I'd probably go and live with my dad, yeah, that is what I'd do."

Okay, maybe mom is trying to come out to her. And she went on to say, "It is not that I don't like gay people, I just think they are gross."

All of these things are going on for this kid, and I just see her working it out. I don't see much creative writing from young kids. I see more when they are older, like seventeen. And the works I see at the writing camp, they still have a lot of learning to do. They have so much to unlearn. They are writing what is "okay." For so many of them, what is okay is "how tragic my life is." Or "how messed up my life is." They don't have a "b" story and "c" story, yet they are still writing what they think adults want to hear.

MA: You should write an epistolary novel about someone writing these letters to you, in which the subtext emerges from her own letters.

JW: I got hundreds of letters on *I Hadn't Meant to Tell You This* [Delacorte, 1994]. So many were like, "I want to know why you wrote this book, I want to know if you know anyone like this, I don't know anyone like this, if I did I don't know what I would do, what would you do?"

I thought, "Oh my God, what are you telling me?" They never say "I identify with Lena," but you can tell by what they are writing.

MA: You've been talking abut the subversiveness of YA books, and about the subtext, and about the subtext of the letters. It is as if there is this underground communication that gets in around the edges of everything else.

JW: For *If You Come Softly* [Putnam, 1998], I get these letters saying "I am just like Ellie." The letters are always from girls, I assume white, not from guys. I just did a residency and sixty kids came up to me saying, "I loved this book, it made me cry, why did you end it that way?" Then adults have a whole different take.

One thing that we as adults disregard is that there are works that, if they get into kids' hands, go straight to their hearts. Our hearts are callused over; we don't want to go there anymore. Our life experiences are so hard, we want a happy ending, while kids want to have these intense experiences. They want to be able to feel that pain because they have that bounce-back potential. They read the book and they are devastated for three hours. It reminds me of what that girl said about the happy ending: "Why can't the happiness take place inside the book?"

MA: It seems to me you've spelled out where YA is for you, but through that, what it is, and what it can be: It is defined by limitations of form and voice that are, really, limitations of access. You get to teenagers via adults, so they need a literature adults can accept. Yet an author can smuggle in to that literature a subtext that matches, that connects with, the limitlessness of teenagers' real experience. So there is this restraint that is really an entry point for wildness. Restraint is confinement that allows access, and restraint is understatement that leaves room for the reader to expand.

And, in reverse, teenagers are having to unlearn the rules of form they half know—intensity as angst—in order to let the kind of multiple-voiced subtext that is in their letters and their lives enter their creative writing.

If the future of YA may press at both ends, at both expression and restraint, it seems there is still a very fertile place where they meet. And borders are continually being redrawn. We see teenagers both spreading out across many forms of media and being receptive to all sorts of inputs at once. I'm happier about the other forms of mixedness in their lives than you are, but we agree this place where wildness and limitlessness meet up with control, concision, and camouflage is the territory of YA literature. I think I can accept that as a challenge.

Index

adolescence: and adulthood, 42, 45; age divisions for (*see* age divisions); coming-of-age novels (*see* coming-of-age novels); culture/era and, 32–33, 75–76; defined, 32, 47, 52; earlier onset of, 58; media and, 34, 41, 45, 46 (*see also* media: and teens); process of, 2–3, 65–69, 80, 112–13 (*see also* *Giselle*); and technology, 47. *See also* teenagers

adult literature: adults' acceptance of teens' reading, 101–3; and censorship, 96–97 (*see also* censorship); coming-of-age novels, 20–24, 35 (*see also* coming-of-age novels); as school reading, 21–22, 36, 42, 47–48, 82, 104–5; as young teens' reading of choice, 9, 41, 58, 70, 101–3

adults: efforts to control YA literature, 42–44, 70, 89 (*see also* censorship); parents (*see* parents)

The Adventures of Blue Avenger (Howe), 133

African-American literature, 35, 100. *See also* multicultural novels

African Americans, 15, 60, 134

age divisions, 8–9, 35–37, 44, 58–59, 62, 110, 119. *See also* YA genre: and age

ALA. *See* American Library Association

Alex Award, 111

ambiguity, 120, 125–27, 134–35

American Diaries series, 67–68

American Library Association (ALA), 9, 31, 54–55, 61, 109, 112. *See also* Young Adult Library Services Association

Am I Blue? (Bauer), 8

Annie John (Kincaid), 21

Appiah, Kwame Anthony, 15, 25

Applebee, Arthur, 104–5

art: artist as Coyote, 95–96; artist as shaman, 80; children's/YA books as literature, 20–24, 71, 75, 77; and multicultural authenticity, 13; in novels, 127 (*see also* graphic novels); teens' experience of, 75, 80–81, 82–83; transcendent nature of, 71, 74, 76–77, 83. *See also* *Giselle; Rite of Spring*

Art Attack (Aronson, Marc), 75, 79

authenticity, 13, 16, 133

avant-garde, 33, 75–76

awards. *See* literary prizes

Babysitters' Club series (Martin), 58

Batchelder award, 110

Bauer, Marion Dane, 8
BBYA. *See* Best Books for Young
    Adults committee/award
Beake, Leslie, 44
The Beautiful Days of My Youth
    (Novac), 44, 92–93
*Best Books for Young Adults: The His-
    tory, the Selections, the Romance*
    (Carter), 31, 119
Best Books for Young Adults com-
    mittee/award, 9, 54–55, 61, 109,
    112, 117. *See also* American Li-
    brary Association
Bible, 86
biographies, 121
bisexuality, 134–35
Blatner, David, 117–18
"bleak" books, 70, 76–77
Block, Francesca Lia, 8, 36, 62
Blume, Judy, 10, 33, 34, 56
Boas, Jacob, 36
La Boheme (Puccini opera), 52
bohemians, 33, 52–53, 75–76
book clubs, 2, 107, 111. *See also* read-
    ing groups
Booklist, 19, 28
bookstores: chain bookstores, 28, 34,
    57; children's bookstores, 8–9,
    27–28, 34, 56–57; problems cre-
    ated by, 8–9, 28, 57; YA section,
    36–37, 105, 131
boys, 45, 100–101, 118
Boys Will Be (Brooks), 90–91
Brooks, Bruce, 10, 35, 56, 87, 90–91,
    124–25
*Bulletin of the Council on Children's
    Books*, 28
Burgess, Melvin, 44, 62, 70

Caldecott award, 110, 114
Carlson, Lori, 11, 36, 61
Cart, Michael, 31, 33–34, 62
Carter, Betty, 31, 33–34, 118–19
Casteneda, Carlos, 10, 34, 53
The Catcher in the Rye (Salinger), 22
CCBC-net, 13, 70
CD-ROMs. *See* multimedia products

censorship, 43–44, 69–70, 87, 89,
    96–97
Children's Book Review, 27
children's literature, 20, 25–30, 56–
    57, 87–89
Cisneros, Sandra, 60, 131
classics, 21–22, 42, 47–48, 82, 104–5
Cleaver, Eldridge, 10, 34, 53
Coman, Carolyn, 25, 26
coming-of-age novels, 4, 20–24, 35–
    36, 77, 124–25
Connecting Young Adults and Libraries
    (Jones), 46
Cool Salsa (Carlson), 11, 36, 61
Cormier, Robert, 35, 56, 75, 125, 127
cover art and design, 56
Coyote, 95–96
crossover books, 20–24, 36, 62, 131.
    See also coming-of-age novels
Cunningham, Michael, 114

Dear America series, 67–68
Denmark, 70
Denti, Roberto, 41–43
diaries, 45, 67–68
Diary of a Young Girl (Frank), 67
diversity. *See* multicultural novels;
    multiculturalism
Donavan, John, 60
Dresang, Eliza, 65

The Ear, the Eye, and the Arm
    (Farmer), 8
Earth-Shattering Poems (Rosenberg),
    67
EDGE imprint, 9, 87
Elkind, David, 103
endings, happy, 132, 137–38
Enzensberger, Hans Magnus, 118
Europe, YA literature in, 41–44, 55,
    63
Everywhere (Brooks), 87

Fabri, Stafania, 47
fantasy, 25, 58–59. *See also* science
    fiction
Farmer, Nancy, 8, 26
fashion styles, 45, 68

Ferri, Alessandra, 73
Festival of the Book (Turin), 46–47
Fleischman, Paul, 82, 120, 125–26, 127
Fogelman, Phyllis, 100
France, 44–46
Frank, Anne, 67
Frenchtown Summer (Cormier), 125, 127
From Hinton to Hamlet (Hipple and Herz), 105
From Romance to Realism (Cart), 31
From the Notebooks of Melanin Sun (Woodson), 136–37

Gaarder, Jostein, 63
Gautier, Theophile, 73
gay and lesbian literature, 35, 60, 62, 88, 94–95, 131, 136–37
Germany, 48
Gibson, William, 47
Gillis, John, 33
Giovanni, Nikki, 36
A Girl Named Disaster (Farmer), 26
girls, 32, 41, 45
Giselle (ballet), 71–74, 76, 82–83
Glashoff, Ilona, 48
Go Ask Alice (anonymous), 34, 55
Golding, William, 104
Goosebumps series (Stine), 58
graphic novels, 59, 63, 118, 136
Guy, Rosa, 131

Haley, Alex, 60
Hamilton, Virginia, 27
The Hanged Man (Block), 8
Harcourt, 9
Hardy Boys mysteries, 58
Hello, I Lied (Kerr), 88
Hersch, Pat, 103
Herz, Sarah, 105
Hesse, Herman, 53, 63
Hesse, Karen, 125
Hipple, Ted, 105
Hispanics, 60. *See also* multicultural novels; Spanglish
history of YA literature, 33–35, 52–63

Holt, 9, 36, 87. *See also specific titles*
homosexuality. *See* gay and lesbian literature; sex and sexuality
Horn Book, 27, 28, 95
horror novels, 58, 63
The Hours (Cunningham), 114
House on Mango Street (Cisneros), 131
The House You Pass On the Way (Woodson), 88
Howe, Norma, 133
Hula (Shea), 21

I Hadn't Meant to Tell You This (Woodson), 137
I'll Get There: It Better Be Worth the Trip (Donavan), 60
identification, 71, 87–89
identity, 8, 15, 15–16, 47. *See also* coming-of-age novels; gay and lesbian literature; multicultural novels
If You Come Softly (Woodson), 137
immigration, 35, 60, 134
In My Father's House (Appiah), 15
integrity, 94–96
international conference on teen literature, 39–49, 51
Internet, 42, 61–62, 70, 92, 106
intimacy, 119
invention, 90–91
Italy, 39–43, 46–48

Johnny Mnemonic (Gibson), 47
Johnson, James Weldon, 86
Jones, Patrick, 46
journal reviews. *See* reviews
Joyce, James, 17, 21, 82–83
The Joy of Pi (Blatner), 117–18

Kaestle, Carl, 10
Kerr, M. E., 88
Kim, Helen, 26, 29
Kincaid, Jamaica, 21
King, Stephen, 41, 58, 70

language: Brooks' use of, 124; culturally "accented" English, 11,

61, 62; identification, 87–89; implicit vs. explicit, 135–36; power
of words, 85–97
Larrick, Nancy, 59
Larson, Rodger, 88, 94–95
Lazzarato, Francesca, 42–44
Letters from the Inside (Marsden), 132
libraries: attracting teen readers, 34,
37, 45–46, 48, 70, 113; avoiding
censorship, 96–97; choosing
books, 23, 26, 28–29, 34, 54, 113,
115, 118–19; in Europe, 39–41,
45–46, 48, 70; reading groups,
61–62; writing projects sponsored by, 61; YA section, 34, 36–
37, 45, 53–54, 56, 59
literacy, 10, 43
Literacy in the United States (Kaestle),
10
literary criticism. *See* reviews
The Literary Mind (Turner), 91
literary prizes, 2, 31, 46, 105, 109–11,
114, 122. *See also* Best Books for
Young Adults committee/award;
Caldecott award; Michael L.
Printz Award; Newberry Medal/
Honor awards
The Long Season of Rain (Kim), 26, 29
A Long Way from Chicago (Peck), 111
Lord of the Flies (Golding), 104
Lord of the Rings trilogy (Tolkien), 53

MacDonald, Ian, 10
magazines: literary reviews (*see* reviews); for teens, 58, 106–7
makeup, 68
Making Up Megaboy (Walter), 127
marketing, 8–9, 28–29, 36–37, 56, 62
Marsden, John, 132
Martinez, Victor, 26, 60
math, 118
McClelland, Kate, 65
McCullers, Carson, 21–22
McMillan, Terry, 10
media: magazines for teens, 58,
106–7; and novel style, 8; and
teens, 2, 10, 34, 41, 45–46, 69, 103,
105, 122–23

Member of the Wedding (McCullers),
21–22
Merlyn's Pen (periodical), 61
Michael L. Printz Award, 2, 31, 105,
109–12, 115–16, 122
Mind's Eye (Fleischman), 120, 125–
26, 127
minimalism, 135–136
Mirabelle, Anne Pissard, 44–46
Momaday, N. Scott, 90
Mondadori publishing house, 43, 44
Monster (Myers), 120, 126–27
morality/moral messages, 79–83,
89–91, 115, 120–21
Mori, Kyoko, 8, 36, 60
Morrison, Toni, 36, 60
multiculturalism, 13–17, 87–89,
133–34. *See also* multicultural
novels
multicultural novels, 8–9, 11, 13–17,
29, 35–36, 59–60, 62, 87–88, 133
multimedia products, 7–8, 10, 92,
106–7, 124–27. *See also* technology
music, 10, 46, 60–61, 75
Myers, Walter Dean, 120, 126–27
My Father's Scar (Cart), 62
mysteries, 11, 58

Nancy Drew mysteries, 58
narrators, multiple/unreliable, 3,
74–75, 81–82, 131–32
Native Americans, 90, 95–96
Newberry Medal/Honor awards, 9,
26, 110, 111–12, 114
New Moon (periodical), 61
New York Times Book Review, 25
Nicholson, George, 56
Nijinsky, Vaslav, 75, 76
Nolan, Han, 26
nonfiction, 118–19, 121
Novac, Anna, 44, 92–93
novels, YA. *See* YA novels
The Number Devil (Enzensberger),
118

obscenity, 130, 132–33
oral literature, 90
Out of the Dust (Hesse), 125

paperbacks, YA, 55–56. *See also* soft-cover publications
parents: book purchasing, 27–28, 54, 131; and the process of adolescence, 66–67, 68, 102–4; and teens' reading choices, 58, 70, 101–4. *See also* adults
Parrot in the Oven (Martinez), 26
Paulsen, Gary, 11
Peck, Richard, 111
picture books, 20, 27
Pinkwater, Daniel, 55
poetry, 60–61, 67, 88, 125. *See also specific titles*
popularity vs. quality, 58, 112–21
Portrait of the Artist as a Young Man (Joyce), 21, 82–83
Printz, Michael L., 109–10
problem novels, 8, 55–57, 60, 62, 71
Publisher's Weekly, 27, 29
publishers: books aimed at older readers, 9; and the boom in children's books, 57; challenges facing, 69–71; and coming-of-age novels, 22–23; and the development of the YA category, 34–35; marketing, 28–29, 36–37, 56, 62; and multicultural novels, 13; myths perpetuated by, 100. *See also* Holt; Mondadori publishing house

quality in YA literature, 29, 114, 116–17. *See also* popularity vs. quality; YA novels: as literature
quest stories, 77

race, 15. *See also* African Americans; Hispanics; multicultural novels; multiculturalism
"Radical Change in Children's Books" conference, 65, 87
Ralegh, Sir Walter, 121
Rapp, Adam, 62
reader-book interaction, 16–17, 90–91
reading groups, 61–62, 106, 107, 112. *See also* book clubs

reading habits, 41–42, 48, 130; adult books, 9, 41, 58, 70 (*see also* adult literature); lack of information on, 106; myths about teen readers, 3–4, 7, 99–106, 118–19; reader-book interaction, 87, 90–91; and technology, 10, 45; variety of interests, 113. *See also* school reading
realism, 79–83, 124
religion, 14, 87
Reveli, Carlo, 46
reviews, 23, 25–30, 111–12, 116, 118–19, 130, 133
Revolution in the Head (MacDonald), 10
Rimbaud, Arthur, 33
Rite of Spring (Stravinsky ballet), 75–76
Roeckelein, Katrina, 127
romance series, 11, 57–58
Romeo and Juliet (Shakespeare), 82–83
Roots (Haley), 60
Rosenberg, Liz, 67
Ruby (Guy), 131
Rushdie, Salman, 96–97

Saint-Georges, Vernoy de, 73
Salinger, J. D., 22, 53
Sapphire, 88
Saving Private Ryan (film), 118
School Library Journal, 28, 29
school reading, 21–22, 36, 42, 47–48, 82, 104–5
science fiction, 11, 47, 54, 58–59. *See also* fantasy
Scieszka, Jon, 9
Send Me Down a Miracle (Nolan), 26
Sendak, Maurice, 27
series books, 57–58, 67–68
sex and sexuality: availability of information, 32, 68–69, 74; novels dealing with, 8, 35, 60, 62, 88, 94–95, 131, 134–35; teenagers and, 2–3, 32, 68–69, 74, 82 (*see also Gi-selle*; sex and sexuality)
Shabanu (Staples), 8

Shakespeare, William, 82–83, 102
Shea, Lisa, 21
Shimmy Shimmy Shimmy Like My Sister Kate (Giovanni), 36
Shizuko's Daughter (Mori), 8, 36
Sisters/Hermanas (Paulsen), 11
Smack (Burgess), 44, 70
soft-cover publications, 9, 55–56
Song of Be (Beake), 44
Sophie's World (Gaarder), 63
Spanglish, 11, 61
speech, books as, 89–90
Spessitizva, Olga, 73
Staples, Suzanne, 8
Starnone, Domenico, 47–48
The Stinky Cheese Man and Other Fairly Stupid Tales (Scieszka), 9
storytelling, 90, 91–92
style, 8, 11, 26–27, 120, 124–27, 135–36
Sutton, Roger, 95
Sweet Valley High series (Pascal), 58

talk poetry, 61
Tan, Amy, 60
Tarantella, Litticia, 41
Taylor, Deborah, 9
technology: access to information through, 34, 68, 69; and the body, 47; and books, 4, 42, 63, 75; and reading habits, 10, 45; and realism, 82. *See also* Internet; multimedia products
teenagers: conflicts and competing narratives, 66–67, 80–81; demographics, 1–2, 11, 34, 35, 56, 60, 62; emotional intensity, 138; exceptional readers, 114; fashion styles, 45, 68; magazines for, 58, 106–7; and the media, 2, 10, 34, 41, 45–46, 69, 103, 105, 122–23; reading habits (*see* reading habits); as reading market, 54, 110–11; school reading (*see* school reading); and sex/sexuality, 2–3, 32, 68–69, 74, 82 (*see also* *Giselle*; sex and sexuality); spaces for, 103; and technology (*see* tech-

nology); worldliness of, 121, 130; writing/publishing by, 45, 61, 67, 92–93, 136–37. *See also* adolescence
Teen Ink (periodical), 61
Tenderness (Cormier), 75
This Beautiful Name Is Mine (Brooklyn Public Library), 61
Tolkien, J.R.R., 53, 58
The Treason of Images (Magritte), 82–83
A Tribe Apart (Hersch), 103
truth, respect for, 94–96
Turner, Mark, 91

Vanishing (Brooks), 124–25
Verri, Paolo, 46–47

Waiting to Exhale (McMillan), 10
Walter, Virginia, 127
war novels, 118
A Way out of No Way (Woodson and Aronson), 88, 129
We Are Witnesses (Boas), 36
Wersba, Barbara, 10, 88
What I Know Now (Larson), 88, 94–95
What Jamie Saw (Coman), 25, 26
Whirligig (Fleischman), 82
Whistle Me Home (Wersba), 88
White, Edmund, 17, 36
The Winter's Tale (Shakespeare), 102
Wollman-Bonilla, Julie, 104
Woodson, Jacqueline, 60, 88, 129–38
Woolf, Virginia, 114
words, power of, 85–97. *See also* language
The Write Stuff (periodical), 61

YA genre: adult assumptions about, 116–19 (*see also* reading habits: myths about teen readers); adult efforts to control, 42–44, 70, 89 (*see also* censorship); and age, 8–9, 19–24, 31–37, 44, 58–59, 62, 110 (*see also* adult literature); breadth of, 8–11; categorization of, 10, 20–24, 34–35 (*see also spe-*

cific categories); death of, 1, 7–11, 56–58; defining, 23–24, 31–32, 33–35, 52, 69–70, 103, 130–31; in Europe, 41–44, 63; evaluating YA books, 3–4, 25–30, 61–62, 109–22 (*see also* reviews); future of, 62–63, 131–34; history of, 33–35, 52–63; integrity in, 94–96; intellectual trends, 15; international conference on teen literature, 39–49; marketing, 8–9, 28–29, 36–37, 56, 62; minority groups and, 59–60 (*see also* multicultural novels); nonfiction, 118–19, 121; popularity vs. quality of, 58, 112–21; publication structures/limits, 130–31; realism vs. morality in, 70, 79–83, 89–91, 94–95, 124; vitality of, 11, 34, 60–61, 110–11; written by teens, 61; YA defined, 52 (*see also* adolescence). *See also* YA novels

YALSA. *See* Young Adult Library Services Association

YA novels: ambiguity in, 120, 125–27, 134–35; challenges facing, 69–71, 74, 76–77; emotional intensity in, 68, 70, 76–77, 137–38; in Europe, 55; experimental novels, 120, 124–27; first-person format,

67–68, 81; function of, 43–44; happy endings, 132, 137–38; history of, 33–35; as literature, 20–24, 71, 75, 77; multiple/unreliable narrators, 3, 74–75, 81–82, 131–32; paperbacks, 55–56 (*see also* soft-cover publications); quality of, 29, 114, 116–17 (*see also* YA novels: as literature); series books, 57–58 (*see* series books); subjects, 8–11, 21, 34, 42, 55 (*see also* problem novels; *specific subjects*); subversiveness of, 137–38. *See also* coming-of-age novels; fantasy; graphic novels; mysteries; problem novels; romance series; science fiction; YA genre

young adult (defined), 23–24, 37, 52. *See also* adolescence; teenagers; YA genre; YA novels

Young Adult Library Services Association (YALSA), 37, 42, 70, 111–12

Young Adult Novel (Pinkwater), 55

younger readers. *See* age divisions; children's literature

Youth and History (Gillis), 33

Zindel, Paul, 10, 56

About the Author

MARC ARONSON is editorial director and vice president of nonfiction content development at Carus Publishing. As an editor, he has worked with authors and artists such as Paul Fleischman, Nikki Giovanni, and Chris Raschka and he devloped and ran an imprint devoted to international and multicultural books for teenagers. Aronson is the author of *Art Attack: A Short Cultural History of the Avant-Garde* (Clarion, 1998) and the award-winning *Sir Walter Ralegh and the Quest for El Dorado* (Clarion, 2000). Aronson holds a doctorate in American history, where his specialty is the history of publishing. He frequently teaches courses on topics including children's publishing, publishing history, young adult publishing, electronic publishing, and publishing and diversity at the NYA Publishing Institute, Simmons College, and the Radcliffe Publishing Program. He lives in New York with his wife, the author Marina Budhos, and their son Sasha.